FLAVOURS OF HALIFAX
and Road Trips

Text by Tom Mason
Photography by Heidi Jirotka

MacIntyre Purcell Publishing Inc.

Copyright 2018 MacIntyre Purcell Publishing Inc.

All rights reserved. No part of this book covered by the copyrights hereon may be reproduced or used in any form or by any means – graphic, electronic, or mechanical – without the prior written permission of the publisher. Any request for photocopying, recording, taping, or information storage and retrieval systems of any part of this book shall be directed in writing to the Canadian Reprography Collective, 379 Adelaide Street, West, Suite M1, Toronto, Ontario, M5V 1S5.

MacIntyre Purcell Publishing Inc.
194 Hospital Rd.
Lunenburg, Nova Scotia
B0J 2C0
(902) 640-3350

www.macintyrepurcell.com
info@macintyrepurcell.com

Printed and bound in Canada by Frisens
Design and layout: Denis Cunningham

ISBN : 978-1-77276-117-7

Library and Archives Canada Cataloguing in Publication

Mason, Tom, 1958 September 27-, author
    Flavours of Halifax : and road trips / Tom Mason.

ISBN 978-1-77276-117-7 (hardcover)

    1. Cooking, Canadian--Maritime Provinces style. 2. Cooking--Nova Scotia. 3. Restaurants--Nova Scotia--Halifax--Guidebooks. 4. Halifax (N.S.)--Guidebooks. 5. Cookbooks. I. Title.

TX715.6.M3835 2018   641.59716   C2018-905670-3

MacIntyre Purcell Publishing Inc. would like to acknowledge the financial support of the Government of Canada and the Nova Scotia Department of Tourism, Culture and Heritage.

"First we eat, then we do everything else."
— M.F.K. Fisher, food writer

TABLE OF **CONTENTS**

Index of Participants   9

Introduction   11

List of Recipes   14

Restaurants and Chefs   19

INDEX OF PARTICIPANTS

Café Aroma Latino	20
Vines Pasta Grill	26
The Watch That Ends the Night	32
Brightwood Golf and Country Club	38
The Press Gang Restaurant and Oyster Bar	44
Coburg Social Bar and Café	50
The Orient Chinese Cuisine	58
Fox Harb'r Resort	66
The Naked Crêpe Bistro	72
Divine Dishes Catering and Gourmet Take Away	76
Harbourstone Sea Grill and Pour House	82
The Carleton	88
Horizons Catering and Spinnakers Restaurant	94
The Barrington Steakhouse and Oyster Bar	100
Sushi Shige	106
Le Bistro by Liz	112
Ratinaud French Cuisine	118
Lot Six Bar and Restaurant	124
Chef Abod Café and Catering	130

A WORLD OF FLAVOURS

The largest port on Canada's East Coast has long been a crossroad for people and cultures from around the world. For almost half a century, immigrants poured through Pier 21 on Halifax's harbourfront, and more than a few of those new Canadians put down roots in the city. Each successive wave of newcomers brought their style of cooking with them — styles that have meshed and melded with the local ingredients to create a uniquely Nova Scotian flavour profile.

Most people think of Halifax's food as seafood — a logical conclusion, as the sea around Nova Scotia provides an abundance of it. Fresh fish and shellfish are brought in daily on nets, lines and traps from nearby communities, including Eastern Passage, Herring Cove, Sambro, Hall's Harbour, and Lunenburg. Today, however, Halifax's famous seafood is as likely to be wrapped in a roll of sushi, or used as a decadent filling for handmade ravioli, as it is to be prepared as traditional, crispy, battered fish and chips.

Nova Scotia has plenty of indigenous food — ingredients that were staples in Mi'kmaq cooking for thousands of years. The blueberry, maple syrup, the fiddlehead fern, and a pungent seaweed called dulse are all distinctly Nova Scotian flavours. So are clams, mussels, scallops, haddock, and Atlantic salmon.

The province's cold, clear waters produce dozens of varieties of oysters, each with a particular flavour and texture. And of course, there's the lobster — arguably our most famous food.

Over the years, Nova Scotian chefs have created some quintessential recipes that have stood the test of time. Seafood chowder began as a pedestrian fish soup in other parts of the world. Nova Scotian cooks added cream and butter and perfected the dish, along with another kind of homegrown chowder — a rich vegetable concoction with the odd name of hodgepodge.

But true Nova Scotian cuisine defies categorization. Planked salmon, rappie pie and blueberry grunt were all invented here, as was the Mediterranean-inspired donair.

Those same winds that have always drawn people to Halifax are today attracting a new generation of chefs. Some hail from places halfway around the world and bring with them the cooking traditions and sensibilities of their homelands. For those who grew up here on the East Coast, they have not only kept the culinary traditions of their home province alive, but have adapted them and given them new life. The result is a Nova Scotia food scene that has never been more innovative or diverse.

Who knows what will become of the lobster, the blueberry, and the clam once these chefs apply their skills and creativity?

— Tom Mason

LIST OF RECIPES

Appetizers

60　Golden Prawns with Steamed Rice

46　Torched Oysters

Soup and Salads

52　Carrot Ginger Soup

120　Cassoulet

132　Fattoush Salad with Grilled Chicken Breast

22　Mexican Chicken Lima Soup

111　Soba Salad with Sesame Dressing

63　Vegetarian Hot and Sour Soup

Bread

122　Pain de Campagne

Desserts

81 Chocolate Pecan Butter Tarts

74 Lemon Curd Crêpes

93 Vanilla Mascarpone Panna Cotta with Lemon Marmalade and Honey Sponge Toffee

31 White Chocolate Peanut Butter Cheesecake

Libations

37 Big Apple, 3 a.m.

56 Espresso Martini

129 Magnum Moon Cocktail with Cinnamon Syrup

87 Spicy Ginger Summer Libation

Main Dishes

84	A New Scotland Supper of Vanilla Butter Poached Lobster with Potato Chive Rösti and Roasted Variegated Carrots
34	Black Olive Gnocchi with Pumpkin Seed Pesto, Summer Vegetables, and Toasted Goat Cheese
40	Buttermilk Fried Chicken and Ribs
114	Coquilles Saint-Jacques
105	Côte de Bœuf
117	Croque Monsieur with Caramelized Onion
90	Fettuccine al Pomodoro
135	Kibbeh Lebaniah
136	Lamb Mandi
102	Lemongrass Ginger Sea Bass with XO Sauce
28	Lobster Scallop Flambé
68	Lobster Stuffed Digby Scallops with Whipped Potato and Celeriac Purée, Chive Oil, and Caviar Beurre Blanc

126   Lot Six Mac and Cheese

78   Moroccan-Spiced Lamb Chops with Apricot Ginger Sauce

48   Pan-Seared Atlantic Halibut with Spanish Dirty Rice, Sautéed Mushroom Butter Sauce, and Roasted Vegetables

71   Pan-Seared Rainbow Trout with Minted Couscous and Brunoise Vegetables

43   Peanut Chilli Rice Bowl

96   Seared Salmon with Acadian Maple Bacon Jam

55   Smoked Turkey Panini

99   Spaghetti Carbonara

64   Szechuan Eggplant

108   Temari Sushi

25   Tostones

RESTAURANTS AND CHEFS

Café Aroma Latino

Chef Claudia Pinto

Claudia Pinto can't remember a time when she didn't cook. Cooking was a family skill passed down through generations in her native Guatemala.

Claudia immigrated to Canada with her family in 1987, at the age of 15. By the age of 17, she was working part-time in the kitchen of a popular Chinese restaurant in Fredericton. When she received her Red Seal chef certification from Nova Scotia Community College in 2004, she already had 10,000 hours of cooking under her belt.

Chef Claudia Pinto with her mother, sister, and niece.

Today, Pinto owns and operates Café Aroma Latino in Halifax's north end. Her combination café and specialty grocery store offers the best of Latin American cuisine. She doesn't focus her menu on one country, choosing instead to prepare delicacies and staples from countries across Latin America, including Mexico, El Salvador, Colombia, Argentina, and her Guatemalan homeland.

"Even though we speak the same language, every country has a distinctive cuisine," she says. For example, while Mexican food is famously spicy, Guatemalan food is quite mild in flavour.

"It was challenging to combine all the flavours of the different countries into something that would appeal to Canadian palates," Pinto says.

To find her recipes Pinto travels extensively, closing her business for three weeks every January to make the journey back to Latin America.

"I travel to experience the styles of cooking that are popular in restaurants, and also the every-day foods that people are preparing in their homes." She brings the best of her discoveries back to Halifax.

"Every item I use in the café is authentic. If I don't have the right ingredients, I don't make the dish." She also sells hard-to-find ingredients at her small grocery store, often catering to Latin American immigrants who are looking to recreate the tastes of home.

"As an immigrant, I know how it feels to find something that I've been missing for a long time. It's a great feeling!"

Mexican Chicken Lima Soup

Ingredients

8 tortillas
1 cup vegetable oil
1 medium onion, chopped
1 jalapeño, stemmed, seeded, and finely chopped
4 cloves garlic, minced
½ tsp ground Mexican cloves
2 sticks Ceylon cinnamon
½ tsp dried Mexican oregano
3 plum tomatoes, chopped
Salt and pepper, to taste
8 cups homemade chicken stock
1 ½ lbs boneless, skinless chicken breast, or boneless chicken thigh
2 green onions, finely chopped
Juice of 3 limes, for the soup
2 avocados, peeled, pitted and coarsely chopped
1 lime, cut into wedges
4 tbsp chopped fresh cilantro leaves

Directions

Cut the tortillas into ¼-inch strips. Heat oil in a medium skillet over high heat. Fry the tortilla strips in small batches, until golden and crisp. Transfer to a paper towel-lined plate to drain. Repeat for remaining tortilla strips. Reserve 2 tbsp vegetable oil.

Transfer reserved oil to a large pot, over medium heat. Add onion, jalapeño, garlic, cloves, and cinnamon. Cook, stirring occasionally, for 3 minutes, or until the aroma is released. Add oregano and cook, stirring, for 30 seconds, then add tomato. Season mixture lightly with salt and pepper and cook, stirring occasionally, for 3 to 4 minutes, or until the tomatoes have softened and released their liquid.

Add chicken stock and chicken to the pot. Bring stock to a boil, then reduce heat to medium. Cook at a slow simmer for 12 minutes, or until the chicken is just cooked through. Remove chicken from the soup and set aside to cool. Lower heat and allow the soup to continue simmering.

When the chicken is cool enough to handle, cut it into a small dice and return it to the pot. Add green onion and lime juice and cook for 3 minutes. Season again with salt and pepper.

Ladle into soup bowls. Garnish with a handful of tortilla strips, avocado, lime, and cilantro.

Makes 4 servings.

Tostones

Directions

Vegetables
In a medium pot over high heat bring water to a boil. Add vinegar, oregano, thyme. Season with salt and pepper. Add the cabbage, onion, and carrot. Cook for 3 minutes. Drain the liquid and allow vegetables to cool for 1 hour.

Filling
Heat 1 tbsp oil in a medium skillet over medium-low heat. Add chorizo, onion, thyme, and tomato, and cook for 30 minutes. Turn heat to very low and keep warm.

Baskets
Peel plantains and cut each into 3 equal pieces.

Heat oil in a medium skillet over medium heat. Fry the plantains on both sides until they turn yellow, but not golden brown. Transfer to a paper towel-lined plate to drain. Reserve oil to re-fry the plantains before assembly.

Using a tortilla press, carefully flatten each plantain until completely flat, but not broken. Each piece should be approximately ½-inch high. Grease 12 muffin tins. Place a flattened plantain in each tin. Use your fingers to press plantain pieces into the tins, to form baskets. The baskets don't need to be very high on the sides. If plantain piece is too small, or if it breaks, use a piece from another plantain to complete the basket. Set aside for assembly.

Assembly
Reheat the cooking oil (used to cook the plantain) over medium heat. Add plantain baskets and fry for 5 minutes, or until golden brown. Transfer to a paper towel-lined plate to drain. Allow to cool for 5 minutes.

Plate 2 plantain baskets per serving. Top each with 1 tbsp of warm filling and 1 tbsp of cold pickled vegetables.

Makes 6 servings.

Ingredients

Pickled Vegetables
1 tbsp vinegar
¼ tsp Mexican oregano
1 tsp thyme
Salt and pepper, to taste
1 cup grated cabbage
2 tbsp finely chopped onion
2 tbsp grated carrot

Filling
1 tbsp olive oil
½ lb chorizo meat
1 medium onion, chopped
1 tsp thyme
1 tbsp chopped tomato

Plantain Baskets
4 green plantains
1 cup vegetable oil

Vines Pasta Grill

Chef Hans Gerstenecker and Tina Gerstenecker

"Cooking is something you have to love doing," says Hans Gerstenecker. "Otherwise it will drive you crazy." It's a love that Gerstenecker expresses at Vines Pasta Grill, the Dartmouth restaurant that he and his wife, Tina, own and operate.

Hans spends long hours every day working the line in his restaurant kitchen, experimenting with new recipes, and edging closer and closer to the perfect cheesecake. "It took me nine or 10 years to get my cheesecake recipe the way I like it," he says.

On weekends he comes in at 1:30 a.m. and cooks through the night so that Vines' popular weekend brunch will be fresh and flawless in the morning. Tina handles the front end of the business, doing everything from managing the dining room to operating a social network that includes nearly 9,000 Facebook followers.

Hans and Tina met in a restaurant. He was working as a chef, and she was a server. They started Vines in 2003 as a partnership and became the sole owners in 2010. The menu is huge. "The main menu doesn't change much," says Hans. "I've tried, but our regulars won't allow it. But I get to express my creativity on tasters' nights, and with our daily features and specials, and our cheesecakes."

His inspiration comes from many places — the traditional German food that his mother cooked when he was growing up, the exceptional chefs he worked with early in his career, and the Italian cuisine that he loves to experiment with.

Vines monthly tasters' nights are hugely popular, featuring seasonal items like Nova Scotia hodgepodge in September, and Thanksgiving pumpkin cheesecake. The Wednesday night pasta bar features salads, Vines' famous Caesar dressing, mussels, soups, and six or seven different pasta dishes.

Every sauce and every dish is made to order. "If someone has an allergy or a food restriction we can accommodate," says Tina.

"With cooking, you can try anything you want," says Hans. "If it works, great. If it doesn't, either modify it, or don't do it again."

Lobster Scallop Flambé

Ingredients

2 tbsp butter
1 tsp chopped garlic
6 scallops
Salt and pepper, to taste
1 claw and ½ tail of cooked lobster
3 tbsp brandy
3 oz tomato sauce
2 oz 35% cream
2 oz baby spinach
4 oz freshly grated parmesan cheese, divided
7 oz cooked fettuccine
Curly parsley, to garnish

Directions

In a large sauté pan, heat butter over medium heat. Add garlic and cook for 1 to 2 minutes, until garlic begins to soften. Add scallops and sauté for 3 minutes per side, until golden brown. Season with salt and pepper, to taste.

Add cooked lobster and sauté for 1 to 2 minutes, until lobster is hot. Add brandy. Cook off the alcohol for approximately 30 seconds. Add tomato sauce and cream. Cook for 1 to 2 minutes, to reduce. Add spinach, 2 oz of the parmesan, and hot fettuccine. Toss to combine.

Finish with chopped curly parsley and the remaining 2 oz of parmesan.

Makes 1 serving.

White Chocolate Peanut Butter Cheesecake

Directions

Preheat oven to 350º F (175º C)

Base
Mix all ingredients until dough stays formed when pressed together. Press dough into 10-inch springform pan. Bake 8 to 12 minutes, or until the edges are brown. Allow to cool.

Filling
In a medium bowl, mix cream cheese and sugar with a hand mixer, until well combined. Add ricotta and mix for 2 minutes. Add eggs, one at a time, until each one is incorporated. Add vanilla, lemon juice, and lemon zest. Mix for 2 minutes.

Melt white chocolate in a double boiler over simmering, but not boiling, water. Temper melted chocolate by adding 1 cup of cheesecake batter to the chocolate and stirring to combine. Repeat 3 times.

Pour the tempered chocolate into the bowl with the remainder of the cheesecake batter and stir to combine. Add peanut butter and stir again. Prepare a water bath by pouring 2 cups of water into an ovenproof container. Place the container on the bottom rack of the oven.

Pour filling over cheesecake base. Bake the cheesecake on the middle rack, over the water bath, for 50 to 60 minutes. When done, the cheesecake should still have a slight jiggle.

Remove cheesecake from oven and run a knife around the outside edge of the pan. This will allow the cheesecake to pull away from the sides of the pan as it cools.

Cool for 2 hours before placing in the refrigerator. Chill overnight.

Ingredients

Base
2 cups graham cracker crumbs
½ cup rolled oats
1 cup sugar
½ cup melted butter

Filling
32 oz (907 g) cream cheese
2 cups sugar
1 lb (454 g) ricotta
8 eggs
2 tsp vanilla extract
2 tbsp lemon juice
Zest of 1 large lemon
10 oz (284g) white chocolate
2 cups peanut butter

Makes 16 servings.

The Watch That Ends the Night

Chef Mark Gray

Head Chef, Janie Bogardus.

Mark Gray always knew he wanted to own a restaurant by the time he was 30.

The Halifax chef and entrepreneur missed that goal by one week. He had just finished his birthday celebrations when the owners of The Watch That Ends the Night approached him with a proposal to take over the business.

Today, the Dartmouth waterfront restaurant, with its spectacular views of Halifax and 1950s hotel lounge aesthetic, is quickly becoming known for its huge collection of beers, wines, custom cocktails, and spirits.

It's also turning patrons on to some unusual fare. "We cure meats and seafood, and we ferment and pickle vegetables; that kind of thing," says Gray.

The original menu at The Watch was focused around the preservation program, but it was a little too "niche" for Dartmouth, according to Gray. Recently, he and his new head chef, Janie Bogardus, have revamped the menu to give it a broader appeal.

"I didn't want this to be a place you only come to on your anniversary or your birthday," he says. "So, we made the decision to put the adventurous stuff to the side, and offer it for special events, instead."

Gray presents themed nights throughout the week — Martini Night Monday, Beer Burger Tuesday and Jazz Night Wednesday — and all of which feature music and dinner specials.

Guests come for everything from The Watch's signature preserve board to the restaurant's hugely popular grilled cheese sandwich. "It's the simplest thing, but a lot of people talk about it," says Gray. Handmade potato gnocchi, tuna tartare, spaghetti and meatballs, and a massive plateau de fruits de mer round out a menu that is anything but ordinary.

For Gray, the decision to take over ownership of The Watch That Ends the Night was made from pure love. "I've been in the industry since I was 15 or 16. I've always known that it would be a lot of hard work and long hours. I felt more than ready to take that on."

Black Olive Gnocchi with Pumpkin Seed Pesto, Summer Vegetables, and Toasted Goat Cheese

Ingredients

Black Olive Gnocchi
4 medium russet potatoes
2 to 4 cups flour (depending on humidity and how moist the potatoes are)
Salt and pepper, to taste
3 egg yolks
¼ cup finely chopped kalamata olives
2 tbsp olive oil

Pumpkin Seed Pesto
¼ cup pumpkin seeds
2 cups basil
¼ cup freshly grated parmesan
2 garlic cloves
Juice of ½ lemon
¼ cup olive oil
Salt and pepper, to taste

Toasted Goat Cheese
1 cup soft goat cheese

Additional Ingredients
Canola oil, enough to cover the bottom of a large skillet
Summer vegetables such as cherry tomatoes, zucchini, eggplant, peppers, shallots
Sliced kalamata olives
Capers

Directions

Preheat oven to 450º F (230º C).

Gnocchi
Wash potatoes and prick with a knife. Place on a baking sheet and bake for 1 hour. Remove potatoes from the oven and let sit until cool enough to handle.

Cut potatoes in half and scoop out the flesh. Discard the skins.

Put the potatoes in a food mill or potato ricer. Rice evenly across a large, clean table or countertop. Cover with a heavy dusting of flour. Season with salt and pepper.

Shape the potato mixture into a mound. Make a well in the middle. Cover with another generous dusting of flour. Pour the egg yolks and olives into the well.

Using a dough cutter or your hands, incorporate the yolks and olives into the potato mixture. Knead the mixture together until a ball of dough forms.

Chef's Note: Depending on the humidity and the potatoes you may need to add more flour. The dough should come together without sticking to the work surface. You want the dough to feel firm, but still be soft enough that it will roll out easily.

Scrape work surface clean and dust it lightly with flour. Cut dough into 8 pieces. Using the palms of your hands, roll each piece into a thin log. With a dough cutter or a sharp knife, slice each log into pieces, roughly 1 cm long. Transfer gnocchi to a parchment-lined baking sheet.

Bring a large pot of water to a boil over high heat. Season water with salt. Add gnocchi in small handfuls and stir gently to prevent clumping. Cook for 2 minutes, or until gnocchi float to the surface. As pieces float up, scoop them out and toss in olive oil. Allow to cool.

Chef's Note: When cooked, gnocchi should be firm to the touch. If it isn't, return it to the water for 30 seconds. To make blanching easier, you can freeze the gnocchi beforehand. Freezing will help to prevent clumping.

Pesto
In a small skillet over medium heat, toast pumpkin seeds until browned.

Place basil, cheese, garlic and lemon juice in a food processor or blender and blend until well combined. Add olive oil in a slow stream, until mixture is loose and thoroughly blended. Add pumpkin seeds and blend until smooth. Season with salt and pepper, to taste.

Goat Cheese
Crumble goat cheese onto a silicone mat and bake for 15 minutes, or until edges start to brown. Stir and spread the cheese at 5-minute intervals, until the cheese is evenly browned. Remove from oven and let cool.

Assembly
Heat canola oil in a skillet over medium-high heat. Add 2 cups gnocchi (1 portion) and toss to prevent sticking. Add summer vegetables. Stir frequently until evenly browned on all sides. Remove from the heat.

Spread enough pesto into each pasta bowl to cover the bottom. Scoop gnocchi into bowl, over pesto. Garnish with toasted goat cheese, olives, and capers.

Makes 3 to 4 servings.

Big Apple, 3 a.m.

Directions

Syrup
In a medium pot over high heat, bring cider to a low boil. Add sugar. Remove from heat and stir until sugar is dissolved. Add fenugreek seed and store overnight. Strain.

Big Apple
Mix all liquid ingredients — except absinthe — in a shaker, over ice. Shake well.

Rinse a cocktail glass with a small amount of absinthe and discard. Strain contents of shaker into a cocktail glass. Garnish with 3 slices of apple, fanned out on a toothpick.

Chef's Note: This cocktail was created by bartender Riley Maggs. It is a perfect drink for both warm summer evenings and cool autumn nights.
Directions

Makes 1 serving.

Ingredients

Apple Fenugreek Syrup
1 cup Noggins unpasteurized apple cider
1 cup sugar
1 tbsp fenugreek seed

Big Apple, 3 a.m.
1 ½ oz Ironworks gin
¼ oz Wild Turkey rye
¼ oz Brennivin aquavit
1 oz freshly squeezed lemon juice
¾ oz apple fenugreek syrup
Absinthe, to rinse the cocktail glass
3 thin slices of apple, to garnish

Brightwood Golf and Country Club

Chef Merrill Perry

Merrill Perry knows his clientele better than most executive chefs. The 1,000 members of Brightwood Golf and Country Club are regular customers after all.

"It's not like a downtown restaurant where customers walk in off the street," he says. "I have a great relationship with the members here. I've gotten to know a lot of them and I've learned what they like."

Nestled in the heart of downtown Dartmouth, Brightwood is a throwback to an earlier age when golf clubs were places to socialize, eat and relax after a round. The picturesque course first opened with nine holes in 1914 and was redesigned as an 18-hole course in 1921 by legendary course architect Donald Ross — the only 18-hole course Ross designed in Nova Scotia.

Perry's stint as Brightwood's executive chef marks a return to his cooking roots. The Dartmouth native first worked at the club when he was 19 years old — one of his first cooking jobs.

His love of cooking began early, at his grandmother's side, helping her prepare Christmas dinners and other meals for the family. He started cooking professionally at 17, attended cooking school and then worked in a variety of pubs, restaurants and hotels throughout Metro Halifax for more than a decade before accepting the job at Brightwood.

Most golfers are looking for basic foods that are nutritious, filling and delicious. Perry fills the bill with items like seafood, Asian inspired cuisine, smoked meats and a selection of home-style barbecue dishes made with house-made dry rubs, marinades and barbecue sauces.

With two restaurants — a pub that offers standard pub fare and a fine dining room offering high-end multi-course meals — Brightwood is a unique opportunity for Chef Perry to practice his broad cooking skills. The club's location in urban Dartmouth also makes it a popular spot for corporate gatherings, weddings and other events.

"I have to draw on all my experience as a chef," he says. "It's a great opportunity."

Buttermilk Fried Chicken and Ribs

Ingredients

Rickard's Red Barbecue Sauce
24 oz ketchup
½ cup Rickard's Red beer
⅛ cup maple syrup
¼ cup white wine vinegar
½ cup brown sugar
½ cup molasses
¼ cup honey
¼ cup soy sauce
1 ½ tsp ground mustard
1 ½ tsp ground ginger
2 tsp sea salt
1 ½ tsp garlic powder
1 tsp chilli flakes

Ribs and Dry Rub
4 lbs back ribs
¼ cup paprika
2 tbsp salt
2 tbsp onion powder
1 tbsp cumin
1 tbsp freshly ground pepper
1 tbsp dried thyme
1 tsp cayenne
1 tsp chilli flakes
1 tbsp brown sugar
2 tbsp fresh rosemary, finely chopped

Braising Liquid
1 cup Rickard's Red barbecue sauce
1 cup Rickard's Red beer
2 cups water
2 tbsp chopped garlic
1 bay leaf

Directions

Barbecue Sauce
Place all ingredients in a large bowl and stir to combine.

This recipe will make a large amount of barbecue sauce. The sauce can be stored in the refrigerator in an air-tight container for up to 3 months.

Ribs
In a small bowl, whisk together the dry rub ingredients. Sprinkle each slab of ribs generously with the dry rub, on both sides. Pat the rub into the meat. Cover ribs in plastic wrap and refrigerate for 24 hours.

Heat oven to 250º F (120 º C).

Combine barbecue sauce, beer, water, garlic, and bay leaf in a medium pot over high heat. Bring to a boil.

Place ribs in a roasting pan. Pour braising liquid over ribs. Cover pan with aluminum foil and cook until ribs are tender, approximately 3 ½ to 4 hours. Remove from oven and allow ribs to rest on a wire rack for 5 minutes.

Heat barbecue to high. Generously coat ribs with barbecue sauce, and place on grill. Cook for approximately 10 minutes, until the sauce is caramelized.

Chicken

In a medium bowl, combine the buttermilk with honey, salt, and pepper. Add chicken and stir to coat. Cover bowl with plastic wrap and allow chicken to marinate in the refrigerator for 24 hours.

Heat oven to 350º F (175 º C).

In a large, resealable plastic bag, mix the flour with the seasonings, and shake to combine. Working with one piece at a time, remove the chicken from the marinade, and allow the excess to drip back into the bowl. Dredge chicken in the flour mixture, coating completely. Set aside on a wire rack until ready to fry.

In a large skillet or deep fryer, heat oil to 350º F (175 º C). Shallow-fry or deep-fry chicken for 3 to 4 minutes, turning once, until light golden brown.

Place chicken on a baking sheet and finish in the oven for 10 to 15 minutes, until the internal temperature reaches 160º F (70 º C).

Assembly

Arrange chicken and ribs on a large platter.

Serve family style, with additional barbecue sauce for dipping.

Makes 6 servings.

Chicken and Marinade

3 lbs boneless chicken breast
4 cups buttermilk
3 tbsp honey
2 tbsp salt
1 tbsp freshly ground pepper

Seasoned Flour

3 cups flour
2 tbsp paprika
2 tbsp Montreal steak spice
1 tbsp onion powder
3 tbsp brown sugar
2 tsp dried basil
2 tsp garlic powder
½ tsp cayenne powder
½ tsp celery salt
½ tsp freshly ground pepper

Additional Ingredients

Vegetable oil, for shallow-frying or deep-frying the chicken

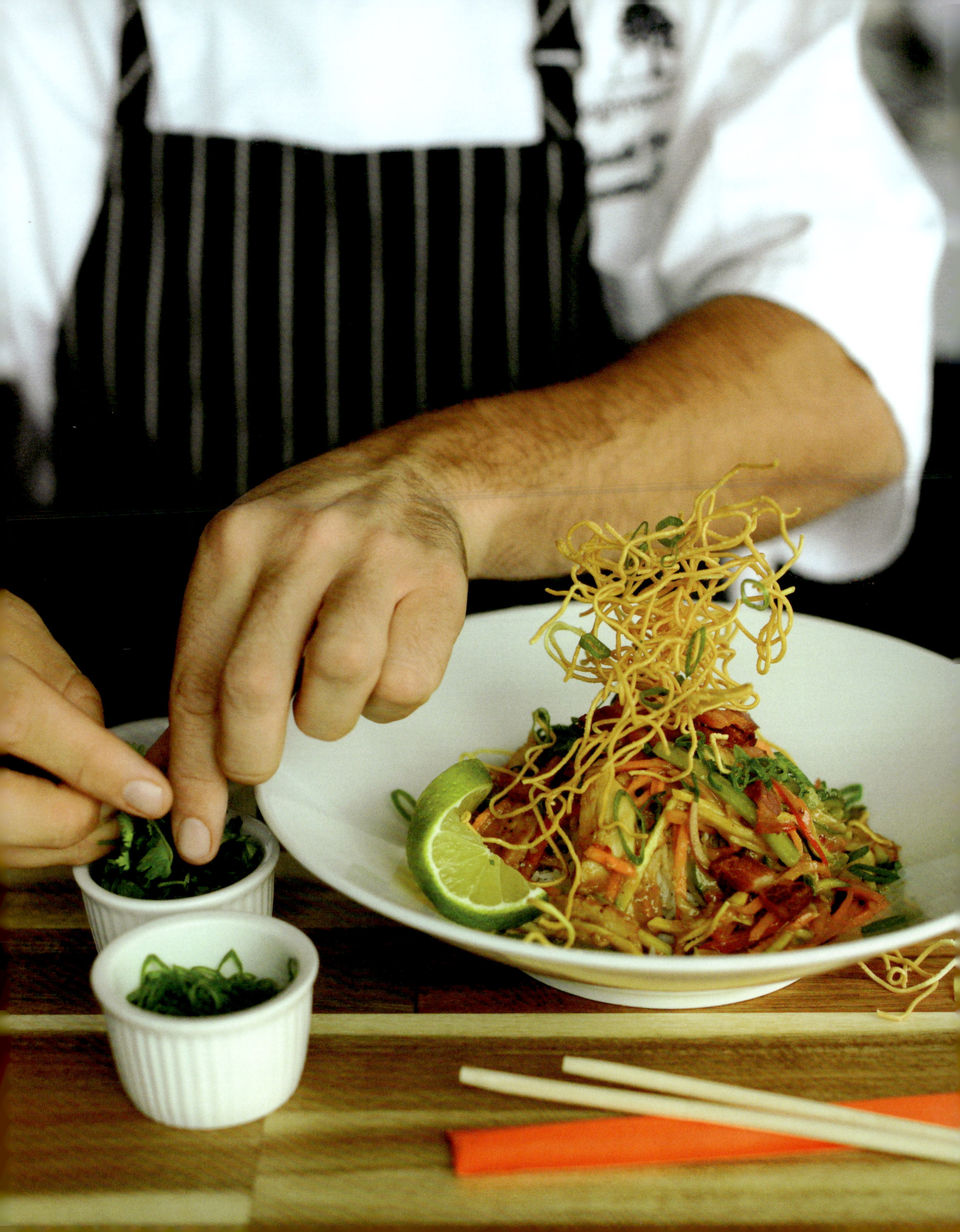

Peanut Chilli Rice Bowl

Directions

Peanut Chilli Sauce
In a medium skillet over medium-low heat, sauté garlic and ginger in sesame oil for 1 to 2 minutes. Add remaining ingredients and whisk to combine. Simmer for 10 to 15 minutes.

Rice Bowl
In a medium skillet over medium heat, cook ginger and garlic in sesame oil for one minute. Add chicken strips and cook until browned. Add julienned vegetables and cook for 2 to 3 minutes.

Add 1 cup chilli peanut sauce and bring to a simmer. If you find the sauce too thick, thin it with a small amount of water.

Assembly
Plate rice in a wide bowl. Top with chicken and vegetable sauce mixture.

For maximum flavour, add garnishes in the following order: cilantro, pork belly or bacon, crispy noodles, green onion.

Makes 6 servings.

Ingredients

Peanut Chilli Sauce
1 ½ tbsp garlic, minced
1 ½ tbsp ginger, minced
1 ½ tbsp sesame oil
2 cups soy sauce
1 cup peanut butter
½ cup rice wine vinegar
½ cup brown sugar
1 tbsp sriracha sauce
1 tbsp sambal chilli sauce

Rice Bowl
1 tbsp sesame oil
1 tbsp minced garlic
1 tbsp grated ginger
2 lbs boneless chicken breast, julienned
1 cup peanut chilli sauce
¼ cup julienned carrot
¼ cup julienned zucchini
¼ cup julienned bell peppers
¼ cup julienned red onion
3 cups cooked jasmine rice
1 tbsp pickled cilantro
4 tbsp fried pork belly or bacon
1 tbsp crispy noodles
1 tbsp green onion

The Press Gang Restaurant and Oyster Bar

Chef Bryan Corkery

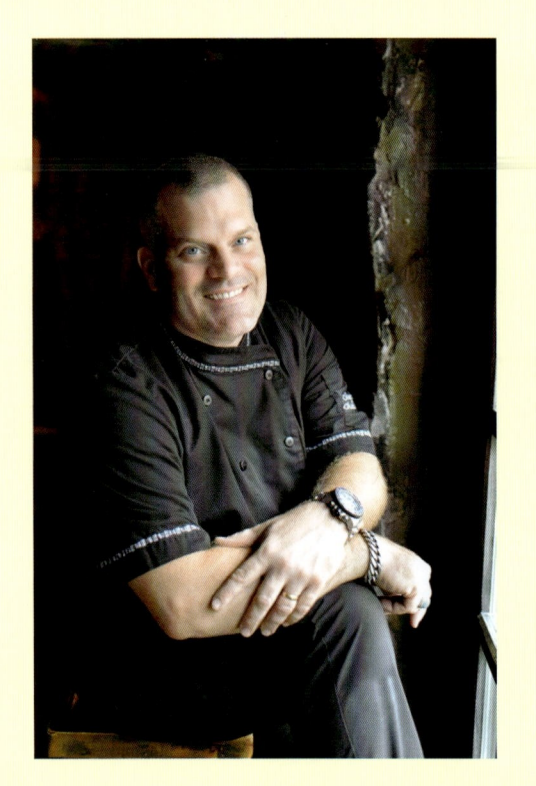

When the rush is over and chef Bryan Corkery has a few moments, he likes to go into the dining room at The Press Gang Restaurant and Oyster Bar and chat with his customers.

"It's the best way to find out how my food is being received," he says. Chef Corkery's dining room forays are part of the approachable, family-friendly style of the restaurant that has been a fixture of the downtown dining scene for nearly 20 years.

"There's nothing stodgy about us," he says. "We want you to feel like you're in our living room."

Call it upscale casual dining. The Press Gang menu features a selection of fresh Nova Scotia seafood, locally sourced meats and produce and — of course — oysters.

Fresh Nova Scotia oysters from Pristine Bay, Hell Cove, and Sober Island are some of the most popular items on the menu. Complementing the menu are a selection of cocktails and fine wines, more than 200 whiskies and Scotches, and live jazz music on Friday and Saturday nights.

"My philosophy is to get the best quality product I can find and treat it properly. I don't mess around with it too much," says Corkery. "I want the natural flavours of the food to do the talking. And I like to offer a full plate — a good, satisfying meal."

Corkery tries, whenever possible, to source locally, but at times that means balancing supply and demand. If something is in limited supply — a one-time landing of red snapper, for instance — he will put it on the menu as a daily feature.

Items that are more consistently available, such as halibut, become core menu items. Corkery has noticed customers becoming more food savvy in recent years, a trend he attributes to the influence of media outlets such as The Food Network.

"Today, not only do our customers want their food to look good and taste good, they want to know where it comes from and who cooked it. It's my job to be an ambassador for our product."

Chef Corkery and staff.

Torched Oysters

Ingredients

Oysters
6 fresh Nova Scotia oysters
Coarse salt, for baking sheet

Filling
1 large Spanish onion, diced
1 tsp olive oil
½ tsp puréed garlic
1 oz Pernod
2 oz baby spinach leaves, finely chopped
Kosher salt and freshly cracked black pepper, to taste
2 oz fine breadcrumbs
1 tsp Italian herb seasoning
2 oz cooked bacon, crumbled
3 oz freshly grated parmesan

Garnish
Coarsely ground kosher salt
Lemon wedges

Directions

Preheat oven to 400º F (205º C).

Oysters
Carefully shuck the oysters and release the inner meat from the top and bottom shell. Discard the top shell and leave the oyster in the bottom shell.

Filling
In a medium skillet over medium heat, sauté onion in olive oil until slightly browned. Add garlic purée and continue to sauté until garlic begins to brown. Deglaze pan with Pernod. Add spinach leaves. Season with salt and pepper and set aside to cool.

Mix bread crumbs with Italian herbs.

Assembly
Add a layer of coarse salt to a baking sheet. The salt helps to hold the oysters in place and prevent them from tipping over.

Arrange shucked oysters over salt. Top each oyster with breadcrumbs, bacon, and a dollop of cooled onion. Finish with parmesan. Bake for 10 minutes, or until parmesan is browned.

Serve warm, on a plate lined with kosher salt and lemon wedges.

Makes 2 servings, 3 oysters per portion.

Chef's Note: For best results, begin by selecting the freshest Nova Scotia oysters you can find. My personal preferences include Pristine Bay, Sober Island, and Hell Cove, all of which are featured at The Press Gang Restaurant and Oyster Bar.

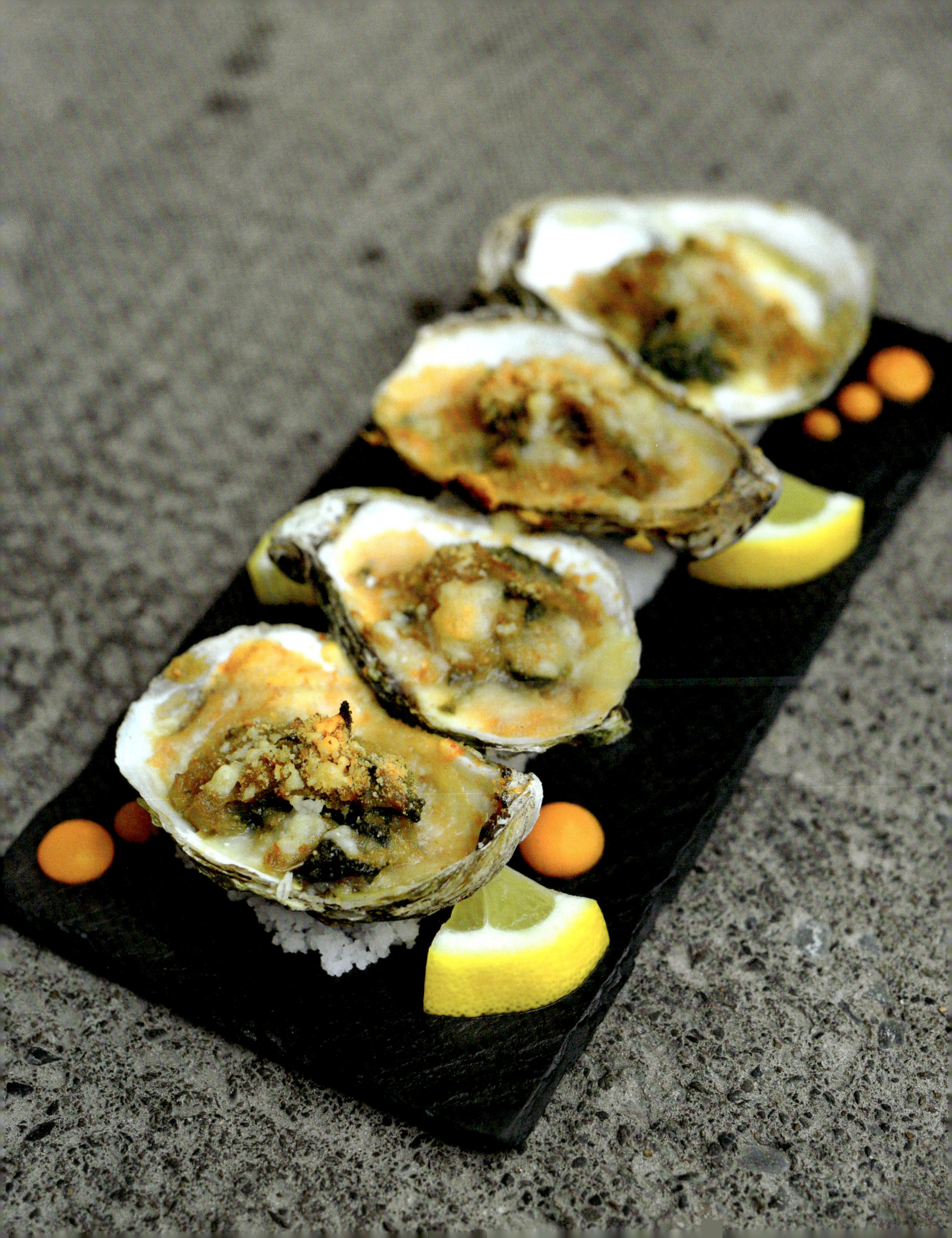

Pan-Seared Atlantic Halibut with Spanish Dirty Rice, Sautéed Mushroom Butter Sauce, and Roasted Vegetables

Ingredients

Spanish Dirty Rice
3 cups water
1 tsp whole cardamom pods
4 bay leaves
½ cinnamon stick
1 cup basmati rice
¼ cup red onion, finely diced
¼ cup celery, finely diced
¼ cup carrot, finely diced
1 smoked chorizo sausage, chopped
1 tbsp garlic, finely diced
¼ cup red wine
1 tbsp paprika
Kosher salt, to taste

Sautéed Mushroom Butter Sauce
½ lb mixed sliced mushrooms
2 tbsp butter, divided
1 oz sherry
Kosher salt, to taste

Roasted Vegetables
2 tbsp oil
1 cup beets, cut into wedges
1 cup baby carrots, whole
1 cup string beans, whole, trimmed
4 heads of Shanghai baby bok choy, halved
1 tbsp butter
Kosher salt, to taste

Pan-Seared Atlantic Halibut
4 (6 oz) centre cut Atlantic halibut fillets
Sea salt, to taste
1 tbsp canola oil
1 oz white wine

Directions

Preheat oven to 400° F (205° C).

Dirty Rice
Bring water to a boil in a large, heavy-bottomed pot. Wrap the cardamom, bay leaves and cinnamon in cheesecloth and tie in a bundle. Add to the boiling water.

Add basmati rice and stir. Cook for 10 to 15 minutes, or until rice is tender. Remove spice bundle and drain excess liquid. Set rice aside.

In a medium skillet over medium heat, sauté onion, celery, carrot, chorizo, and garlic. Deglaze pan with red wine. Stir in paprika. Combine mixture with cooked rice and season with salt. Set aside for assembly.

Mushroom Butter Sauce
In a medium skillet over medium heat, sauté the mushrooms in 1 tbsp butter, until tender. Deglaze pan with sherry. Add remaining 1 tbsp butter and swirl. Season with salt. Set aside for assembly.

Vegetables
Spread beets and carrots on a large baking sheet, Drizzle with oil and toss to coat. Roast for 35 to 40 minutes, stirring every 10 minutes, or until vegetables are cooked through and browned. Set aside for assembly.

Shortly before service, bring a medium pot of salted water to a boil over high heat. Add beans and bok choy and cook for 3 to 4 minutes, or until just tender. Drain vegetables and toss with butter and a pinch of salt.

Halibut
Season halibut fillets with sea salt.

In a heavy skillet over high heat, heat canola oil until very hot. There should be wisps of smoke coming from the pan. Carefully place seasoned fish in skillet. It is important to use caution, as the oil may flash with fire.

Do not disturb the halibut while it sears. When the edges begin to brown, turn the fish over.

Deglaze skillet with white wine. Again, use caution, as the pan may flash with fire.

Remove pan from heat and place in oven for 6 to 7 minutes.

Assembly
Place a mound of rice in the centre of the plate. Arrange cooked vegetables around the rice. Place halibut fillet over rice, and top with mushroom butter sauce.

Makes 4 servings.

Chef's Note: I like to use a variety of mushrooms for this sauce: cremini, portabella, shiitake, and oyster are some of my favourites.

Coburg Social Bar and Café

Kelly Irvine and Jane Merchant

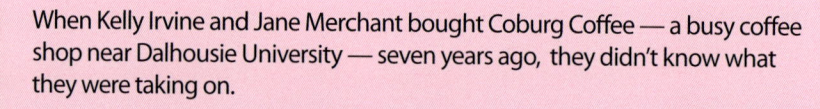

When Kelly Irvine and Jane Merchant bought Coburg Coffee — a busy coffee shop near Dalhousie University — seven years ago, they didn't know what they were taking on.

"It was a very steep learning curve," Irvine admits. "We made a few mistakes along the way. But we did it!"

Jane Merchant and Kelly Irvine.

Under the careful guidance of its owners, the recently renamed Coburg Social Bar and Café has evolved into something unique in Halifax's South End. For Dalhousie students and faculty, it has become a preferred place to gather and to hold meetings. The restaurant has become well known for serving some of the most delicious comfort foods, sandwiches, and baked goods in town. And Coburg Social's recently acquired liquor license has transformed the café into a popular neighbourhood watering hole.

Irvine and Merchant concentrate on delivering delicious and nutritious food: paninis packed with fresh, healthy ingredients; overnight oats; breakfast sandwiches; and burritos filled with beans, rice, avocado, and cheese. Avocado toast made with almond butter and organic, locally sourced bread is Coburg Social's top-selling item, while specialty coffees and baked goods are also popular.

The owners have recently added evening table service to the mix. "We've kept our lunch menu and developed an entirely new menu for the evening," says Irvine.

The restaurant has also begun offering a wide selection of beer, wine, and cocktails. Irvine's son, Williston, a professional bartender, developed Coburg Social's unique cocktail program.

"I think we've done an excellent job at having something for everyone here, and having the best products," she says.

The renovations, menu redevelopment, and rebranding took three years of hard work, but Irvine says the most critical part of the effort was making sure that Coburg Social maintained its casual and inviting ambiance.

"We named it Coburg Social Bar and Café for a reason," she says. "We strive to create a space that is welcoming — a place to meet up with your friends, relax, and feel like you are part of something."

Carrot Ginger Soup

Ingredients

1 tbsp olive oil
1 onion, diced
3 cloves garlic, minced
Salt, pepper, and red pepper flakes, to taste
2 tbsp grated fresh ginger
6 to 8 medium carrots, sliced
2 stalks of celery, diced
2 potatoes, chopped
8 cups vegetable broth
14 oz can of coconut milk
Sour cream, to garnish
Parsley, to garnish

Directions

Heat oil in large pot over medium-high heat. Add onion, garlic, salt, pepper, and red pepper flakes. Sauté until onion is translucent. Stir in ginger, carrots, and celery. Sauté for 5 minutes. Add potatoes and broth. Bring to a boil, cover and simmer until vegetables are soft.

Using a blender or immersion blender, purée until smooth. Add more broth, as needed, until desired consistency is achieved.

Add coconut milk and mix well.

Ladle into soup bowls. Garnish with sour cream and parsley.

Makes 6 servings.

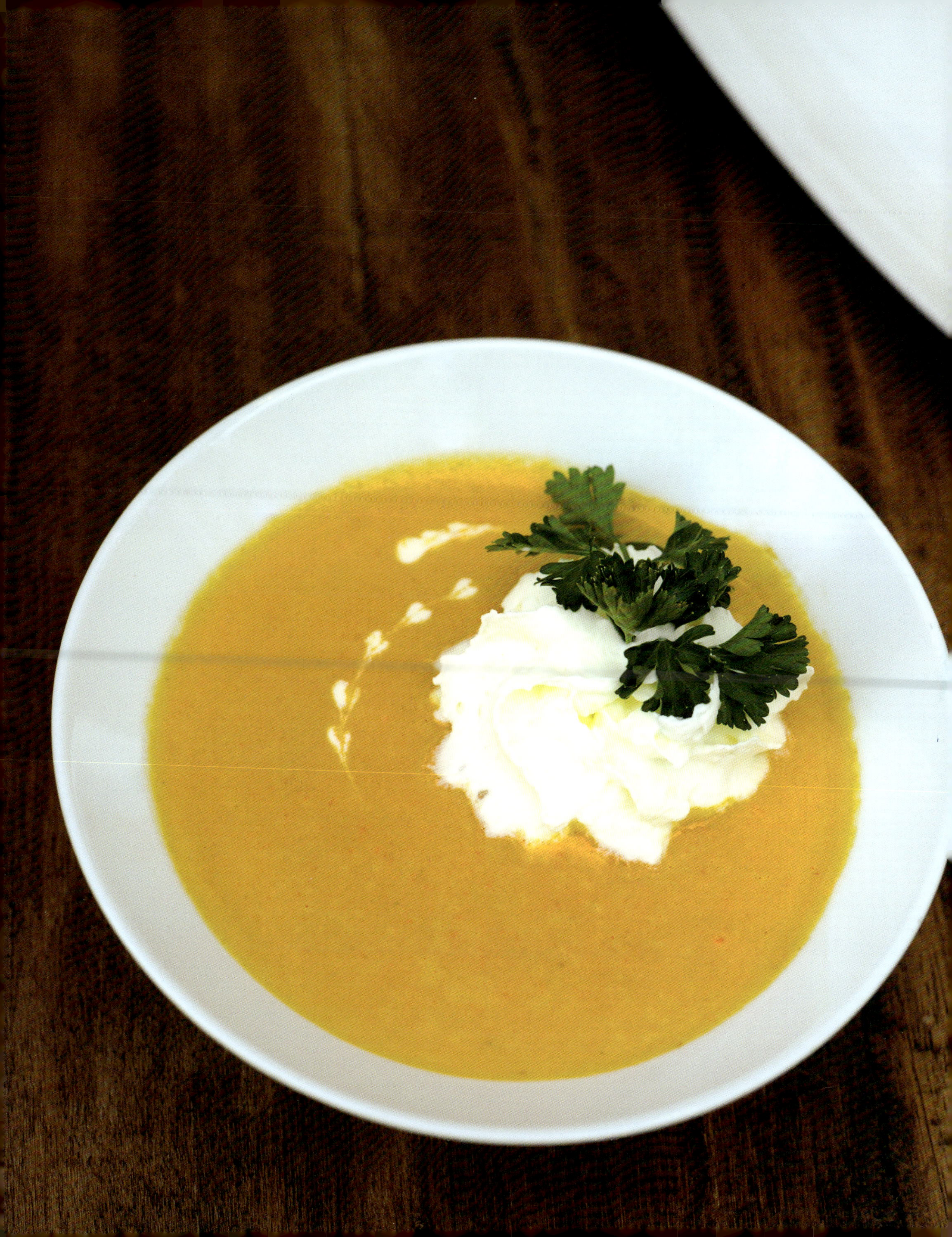

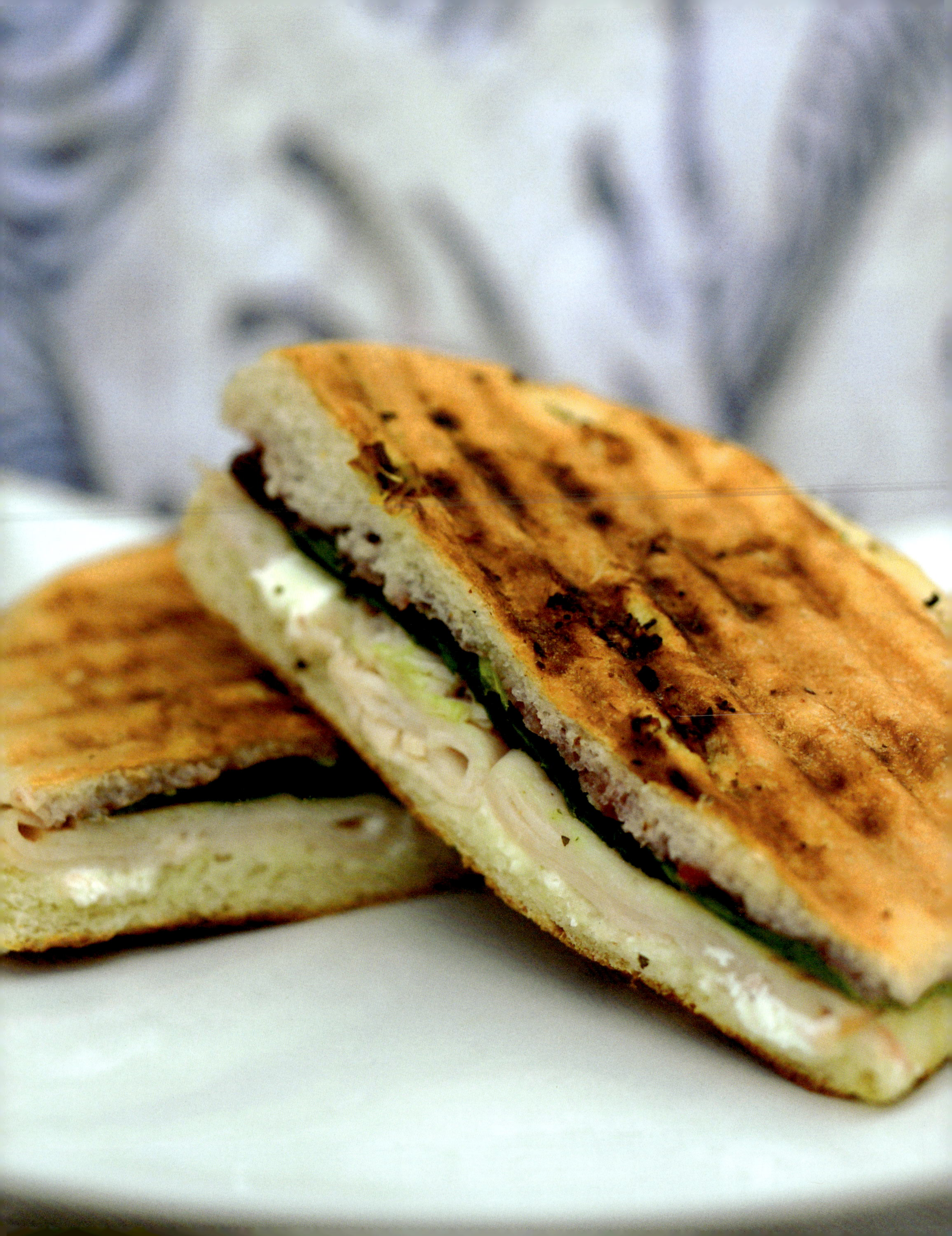

Smoked Turkey Panini

Directions

Cut bun in half and spread liberally with mayonnaise.

Layer remaining ingredients on the bun. Grill in a panini press until the bun is warm and the cheese has melted.

Slice panini in half and plate.

Makes 1 serving.

Ingredients

Rosemary garlic focaccia bun
1 tbsp mayonnaise
3 slices smoked turkey
2 tbsp crumbled goat cheese
1 tbsp cranberry sauce
Handful of baby spinach

Espresso Martini

Ingredients

1 ½ oz blanco tequila
½ oz Kahlua
¼ oz Patrón XO Cafe
1 oz espresso
Ice
Ground espresso, to garnish

Directions

Mix tequila, Kahlua, Patrón, and espresso in a shaker, over ice. Shake well.

Double strain into a 5 ½ oz coupe glass. Garnish with ground espresso.

Makes 1 serving.

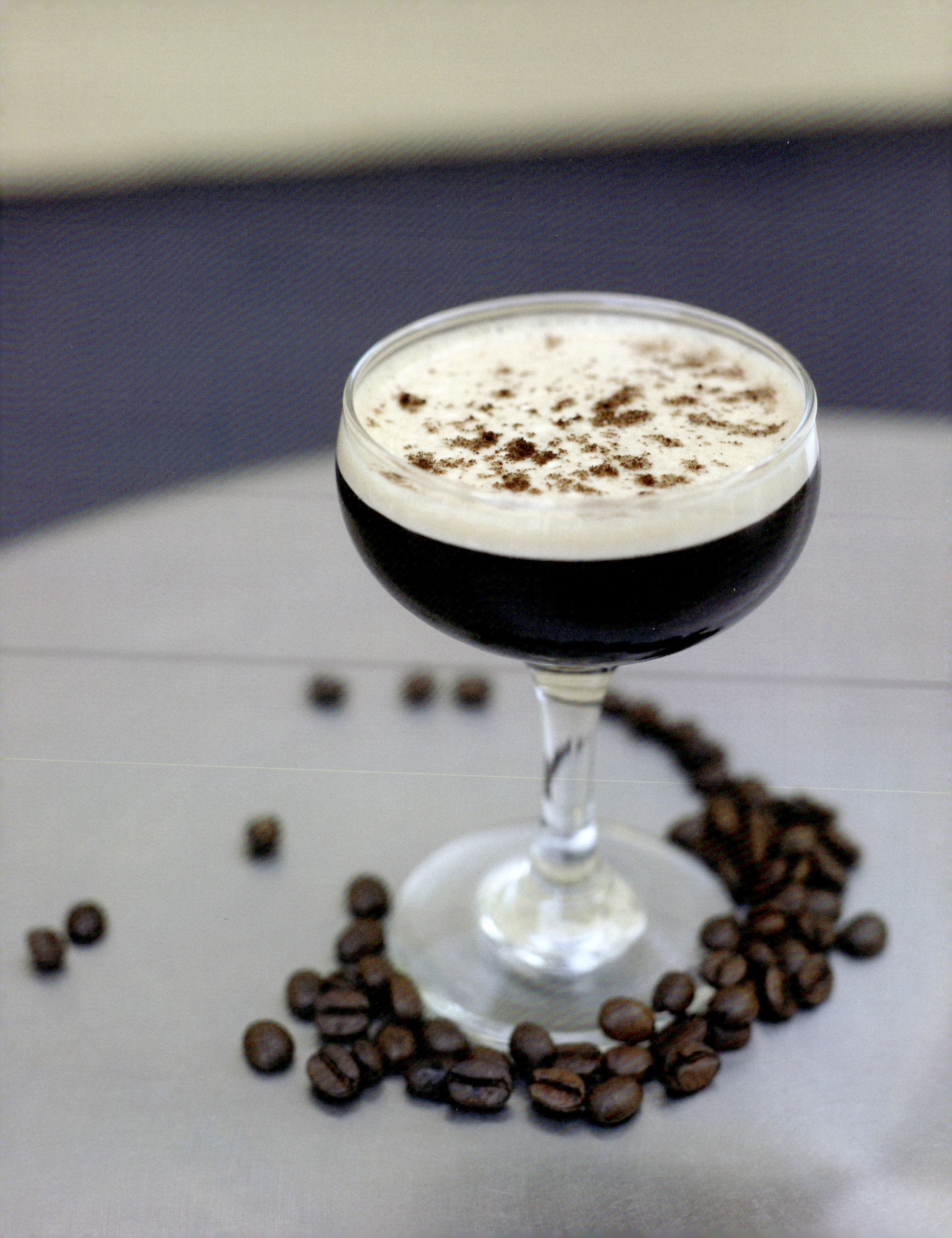

The Orient Chinese Cuisine

Chef Ivan Chan

Chef Ivan Chan has one overarching goal for his restaurant, The Orient, on the Bedford Highway: he wants to introduce Halifax to the subtleties and complexities of the food of his homeland.

"I've always felt there was a level of Chinese fine dining that is missing in North America," he says.

Chan grew up in Hong Kong while the small nation was still under British rule. Even as a child, he had strong ties to cuisine. He learned to cook by helping his grandmother, a prep cook in one of the top restaurants in Hong Kong, as she hosted weekly dinners for about 20 family members. His father was one of the city's premier interior designers, who counted many of Hong Kong's best restaurants as his clients.

Ivan immigrated to Canada with his family in the early 1990s and studied computer science at Dalhousie University. He started his own computer repair business after graduation, but he couldn't shake his love for cooking.

"I wanted to turn my passion for food and cooking into a career," he says. In 2010 he finally opened his restaurant in Halifax.

Today, Chan is internationally recognized, with a string of awards for his cooking. He focuses on Cantonese cuisine, sourcing most of his ingredients from local farmers and fishermen.

"Good Cantonese cooking is all about the freshness and flavour of the ingredients," he says. "I don't have a walk-in freezer. Everything comes in fresh and gets used right away."

He uses a minimal amount of salt and no soy sauce in most of his dishes, and he doesn't coat his food with batter. "I don't have anything against chicken balls or that type of Chinese cooking. It's just not what I do," he says. "Everything I serve is made in-house, from scratch, and cooked to order."

Chan admits that running The Orient restaurant is an all-consuming enterprise, but says he wouldn't have it any other way. "My reward comes when people like my food. That's what drives me."

Golden Prawns with Steamed Rice

Ingredients

14 to 18 oz medium shrimp (prawns), with shell
Pinch of salt
3 to 4 pieces salted duck egg yolk (available at Asian grocery stores)
2 cups oil, for frying
Cornstarch, enough to dust shrimp
1 tbsp unsalted butter
2 cups steamed white rice

Directions

Trim and devein the shrimp, leaving shells attached. To devein, cut a slit along the back of the shrimp. Remove and discard the vein that runs along the back, then rinse and drain shrimp.

Season with salt. The salt will help to remove excess moisture from the shrimp.

Steam duck egg yolks over medium heat for 15 minutes.

Heat oil in a large wok, over high heat. Lightly coat shrimp with cornstarch, to seal in moisture. Deep-fry in hot oil for 3 minutes, or until light golden brown. Remove from wok and place on a paper towel-lined plate.

Drain all but 1 tbsp of oil from the wok and reduce heat to low. Add butter and salted egg yolk. Use a spatula to crush the yolk and cook for 20 seconds, or until the aroma is released. The crushed yolk will have a sandy texture. This is known in Asian cooking as "golden sand."

Reduce heat to minimum and allow the wok to cool before adding shrimp to the yolk mixture. Cook briefly, for only 15 to 20 seconds, while tossing to coat shrimp in egg yolk "sand."

Plate rice on a platter, and top with shrimp.

Serve family style.

Makes 3 to 4 appetizer servings.

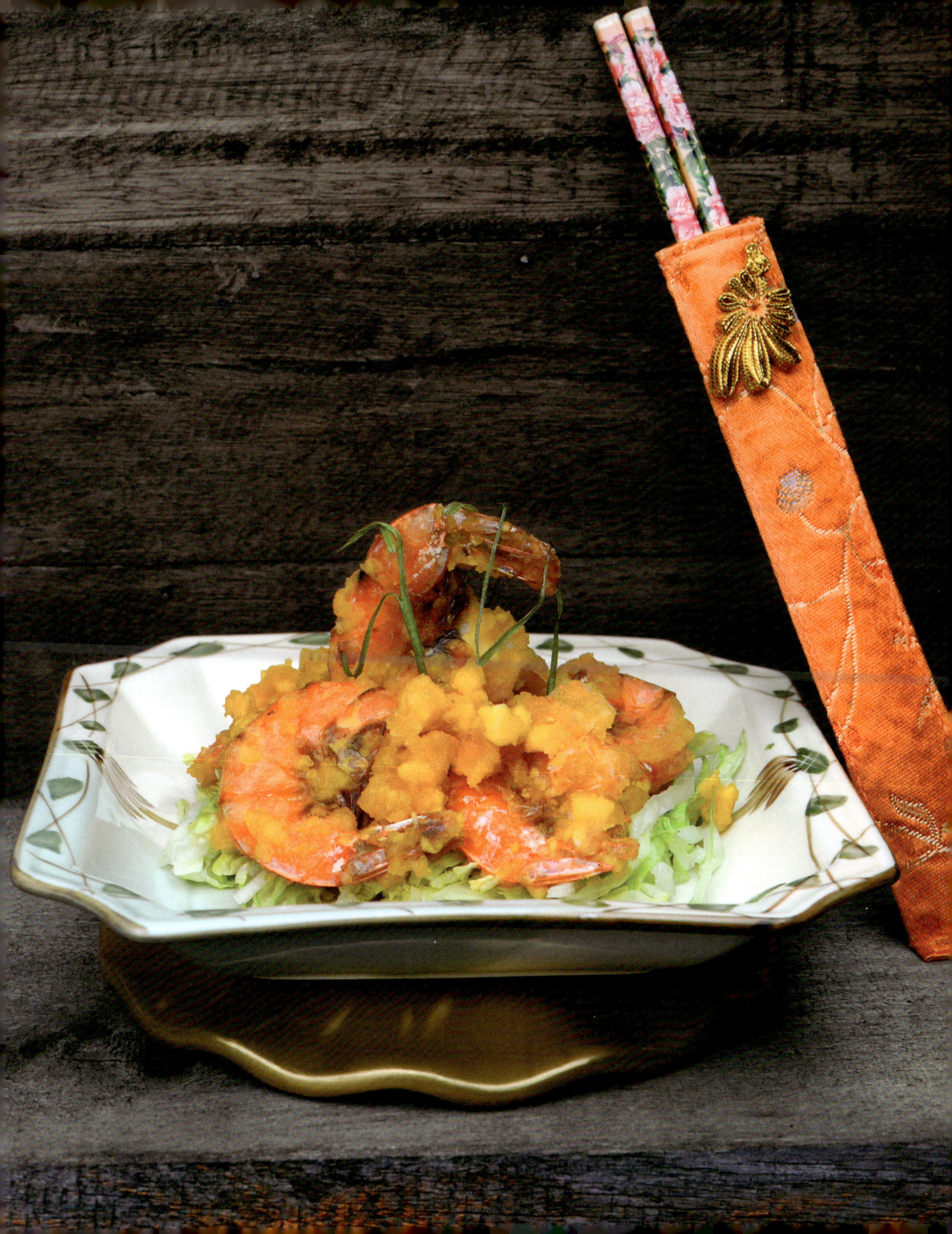

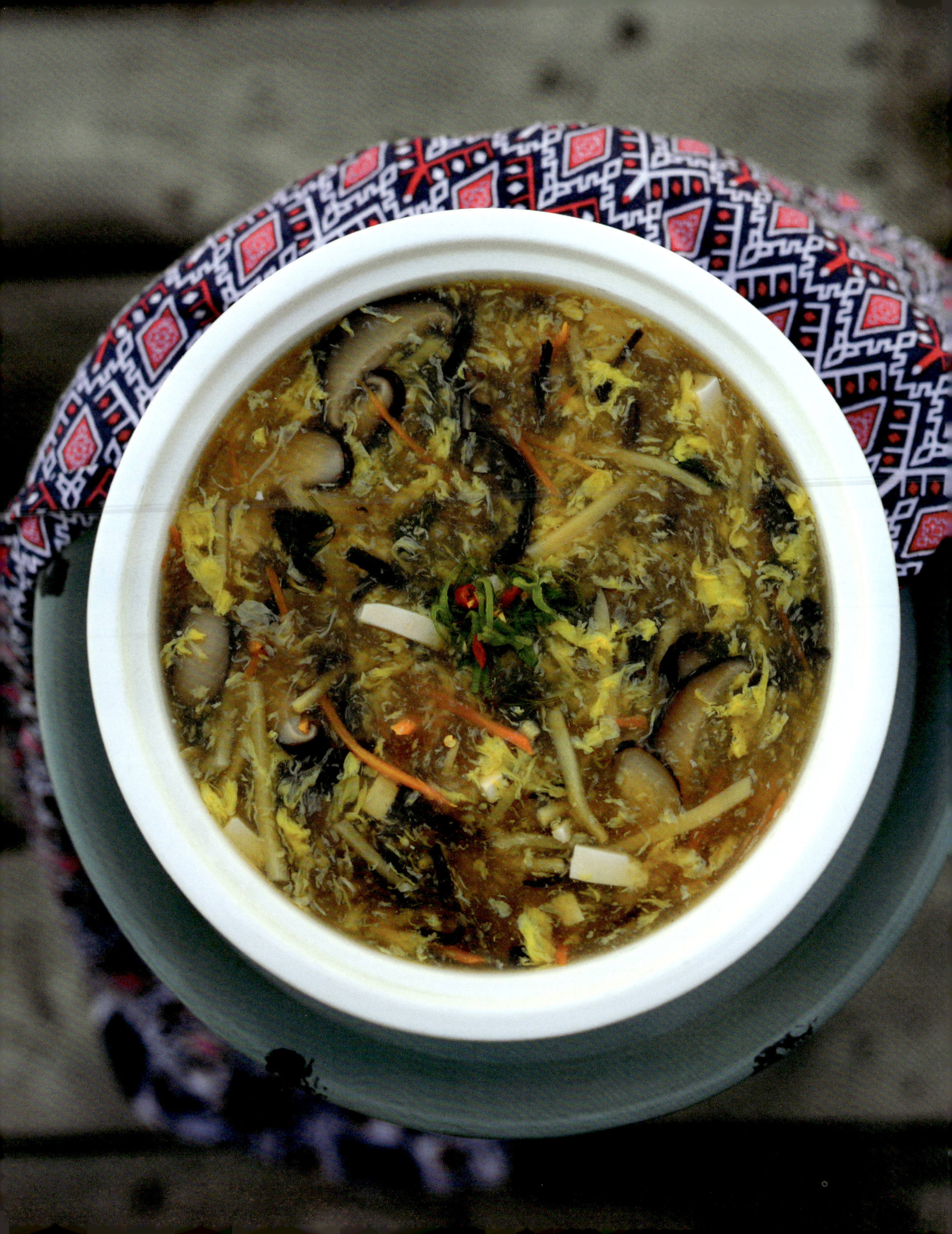

Vegetarian Hot and Sour Soup

Directions

Soak the dried wood ear and shiitake mushrooms for 1 to 2 hours, to rehydrate. Drain. Roughly chop the wood ears and slice the shiitake mushrooms.

Bring the stock to a boil in a large wok or pot over high heat. Add vinegar, chilli oil, and white pepper.

Reduce heat to medium. Add mushrooms, carrot, and bamboo shoots, and simmer for 5 minutes, to infuse the flavours into the stock.

Mix cornstarch and water and stir until completely dissolved.

Use a soup ladle to stir the soup steadily in a circular motion, to create a whirlpool. In a thin stream, slowly pour three-quarters of the cornstarch mixture into the whirlpool. Check the consistency of the soup. It should be thick enough to coat the ladle. If not, continue to stir and add additional cornstarch mixture.

When soup has reached the desired consistency, add the tofu and stir to combine.

Beat eggs in a small bowl. Repeat the whirlpool technique to incorporate the beaten eggs. This will create beautiful swirls of egg in the soup.

Season soup lightly with salt and garnish with scallions.

Serve in a soup tureen, family style.

Makes 3 to 4 servings.

Ingredients

¼ cup dried wood ear mushrooms
¼ cup dried shiitake mushrooms
8 cups vegetable stock
3 teaspoon Chinkiang vinegar (available at Asian grocery stores)
1 teaspoon chilli oil
½ teaspoon freshly ground white pepper
¼ cup shredded carrot
¼ cup shredded bamboo shoots
¼ cup cornstarch
¼ cup water
¼ cup medium-firm tofu, cut into 2-inch x ¼-inch x ¼-inch strips
2 eggs
Pinch of salt, to taste
2 tbsp chopped green onion, to garnish

Szechuan Eggplant

Ingredients

Eggplant
16 oz eggplant
1 tbsp salt
4 cups water
2 cups oil, for frying

Sauce
1 tbsp ginger, chopped
1 tbsp garlic, grated
2 tbsp green onion, chopped
1 tbsp chilli bean sauce
1 tbsp hoisin sauce
3 ½ oz minced pork
1 tbsp cooking wine
2 tsp sugar
2 tbsp water
Pinch of salt, to taste

Additional Ingredients
Julienned green onion, to garnish

Directions

Eggplant
Trim ends from the eggplants. Cut into 1-inch x 1-inch x 3-inch strips. Soak in salted water for 15 minutes. Drain and pat dry with paper towel. In a large wok, heat oil to 350º F (175º C). Deep fry eggplant for 2 minutes, or until lightly browned. Remove eggplant and drain on a paper towel-lined plate.

Sauce
Reserve 2 tbsp oil in the wok. Reduce heat to medium. Stir-fry ginger, garlic, green onion, chilli bean sauce, and hoisin sauce for 1 minute.

Add minced pork, and cook for 1 to 2 minutes, stirring frequently. Add wine, sugar, 2 tbsp of water, and pinch of salt. Bring to a simmer.

Reduce heat to low. Add eggplant and braise for 20 seconds, while stirring to coat eggplant with sauce.

Assembly
Place eggplant and sauce on a large plate and garnish with julienned green onion.

Serve family style.

Makes 3 to 4 servings.

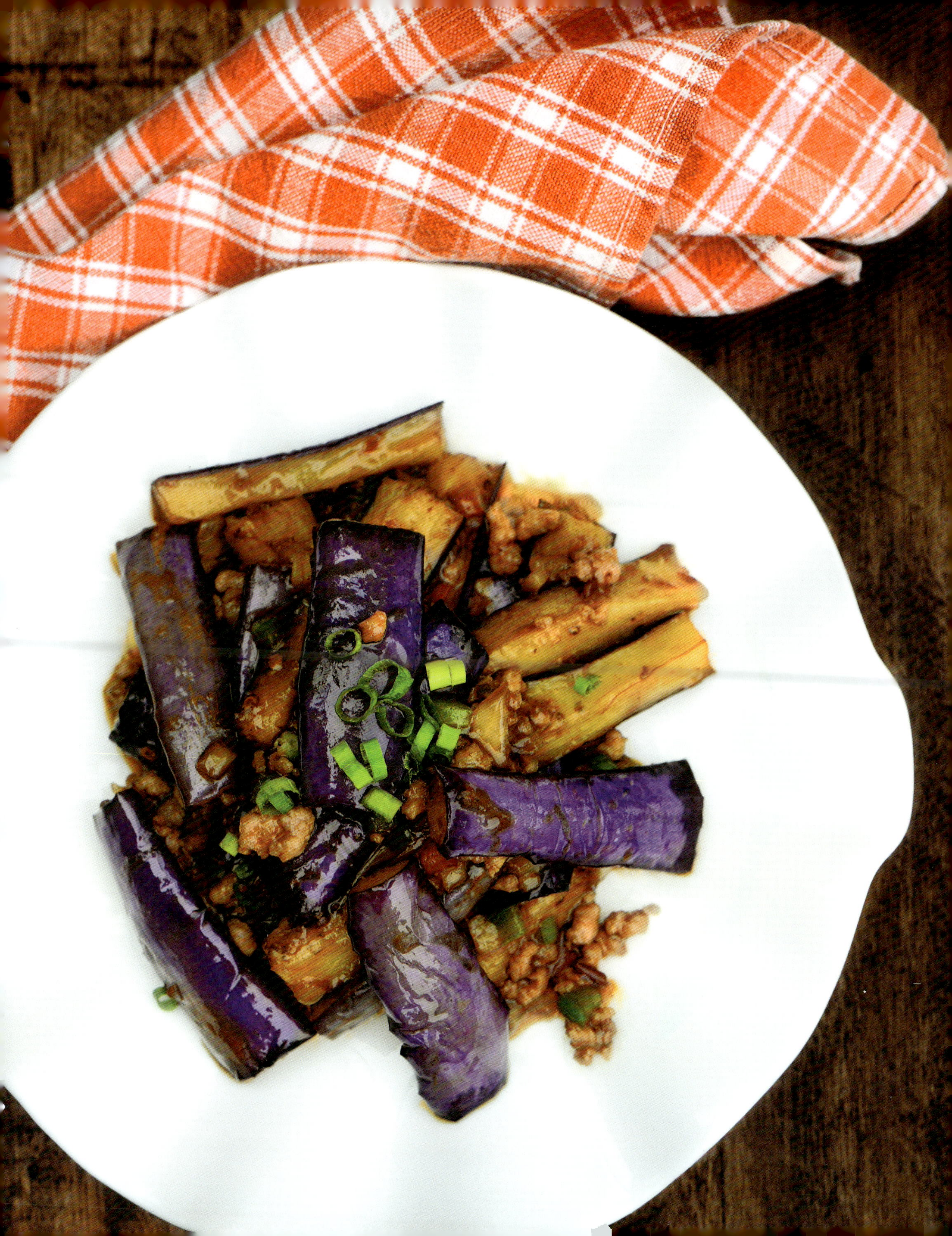

Fox Harb'r Resort

Chef Shane Robilliard

For Shane Robilliard, a trip to one of Fox Harb'r Resort's well-stocked trout ponds is part of the daily routine. Once there, Chef Robilliard casts a line into the water to catch the fresh rainbow trout he serves as part of Fox Harb'r's menu.

To Robilliard, working as executive chef at the upscale resort on Nova Scotia's Northumberland Strait means having access to all kinds of fresh ingredients. Fox Harb'r resort has its own horticulturalist who grows a variety of vegetables and herbs, including many of the peppers, tomatoes, eggplant, and onions that the restaurant serves. The resort also has apple orchards and vineyards.

"The resort is at about 70 per cent sustainability in lettuce, and 50 to 60 per cent in herbs," says Robilliard. "This is a unique opportunity for me to work with food that is fresh out of the garden."

That bounty often dictates Robilliard's menu choices.

"When the tomatoes are at their peak, we have to use them. That means soups, salads, entrées; everything I can think of with tomatoes in it. Right now, I'm working with eggplant."

Set in the midst of a spectacular oceanside 18-hole golf course, Fox Harb'r is a private resort that features a deepwater marina, which can accommodate yachts of 80 feet or more. It also has a private jetport with a 5,000-foot serviced runway and aircraft hangar. Fox Harb'r is luxurious and upscale, but Robilliard says there's nothing pretentious about his recipes.

"The clientele at Fox Harb'r expects the best — the best quality, the best local ingredients. That's what I focus on, but at the same time I try to keep things simple."

A native of British Columbia, Robilliard started cooking professionally shortly after graduating from high school.

"Throughout my career, I've taken every opportunity to eat cool food and prepare cool food. I love exploring the great seafood and other fresh food that's available here on the East Coast. I'm very fortunate that Nova Scotia has been so welcoming."

Lobster Stuffed Digby Scallops with Whipped Potato and Celeriac Purée, Chive Oil, and Caviar Beurre Blanc

Ingredients

Chive Oil
1 small bunch of chives
6 oz olive oil

Whipped Potato and Celeriac Purée
2 large potatoes, peeled and diced
1 small head of celeriac, peeled and diced
3 ½ oz 35% cream
2 oz unsalted butter
Salt and pepper, to taste

Caviar Beurre Blanc
1 shallot, finely diced
1 tbsp olive oil
1 cup white wine
4 oz unsalted butter
Salt and pepper, to taste
¼ oz caviar

Lobster Stuffed Digby Scallops
4 Digby scallops, U10 or larger
2 oz cooked lobster, chopped
1 oz cream cheese
Salt and pepper, to taste
1 tbsp canola or grapeseed oil

Additional Ingredients
Seasonal vegetables
Fresh herbs or microgreens, to garnish

Directions

Chive Oil
Place the chives in a blender with 3 oz of the olive oil. Blend well. Add the remaining 3 oz of oil and blend again. Let stand for 1 hour. Strain through cheesecloth.

Chive oil should be bright green in colour.

Purée
In a medium pot over high heat, boil potatoes and celeriac until tender. Drain.

Press vegetables through a ricer. Add cream and butter and mix well. Season with salt and pepper.

Beurre Blanc
In a medium saucepan over medium heat, sauté shallots in olive oil. Add white wine. Cook until the wine is reduced by two-thirds.

Reduce heat to low. Add butter and whisk until well incorporated.

Remove from heat and strain to remove shallots. Season with salt and pepper. Remember that caviar is a bit salty - do not over season the sauce.

Fold in the caviar at the last moment, so that it remains fresh.

Scallops
Make a large slice in the side of the scallops, to open.

Mix chopped lobster and cream cheese. Season with salt and pepper.

Stuff scallops with lobster mixture, and fold to close. Chill in refrigerator for 30 minutes.

In a medium skillet over very high heat, heat canola or grapeseed oil until oil begins to smoke. Add scallops and sear for approximately 2 minutes per side, until a golden crust forms on each side.

The lobster and cream cheese stuffing will warm as scallops cook. Be careful not to overcook, as cream cheese will melt.

Assembly
Spoon 4 oz of the purée into the middle of the plate. Arrange seasonal vegetables around the edge of the plate. Place 4 scallops on top of the purée. Spoon beurre blanc over scallops and vegetables. Drizzle with chive oil, and garnish with a sprig of herb or microgreens.

Makes 2 servings.

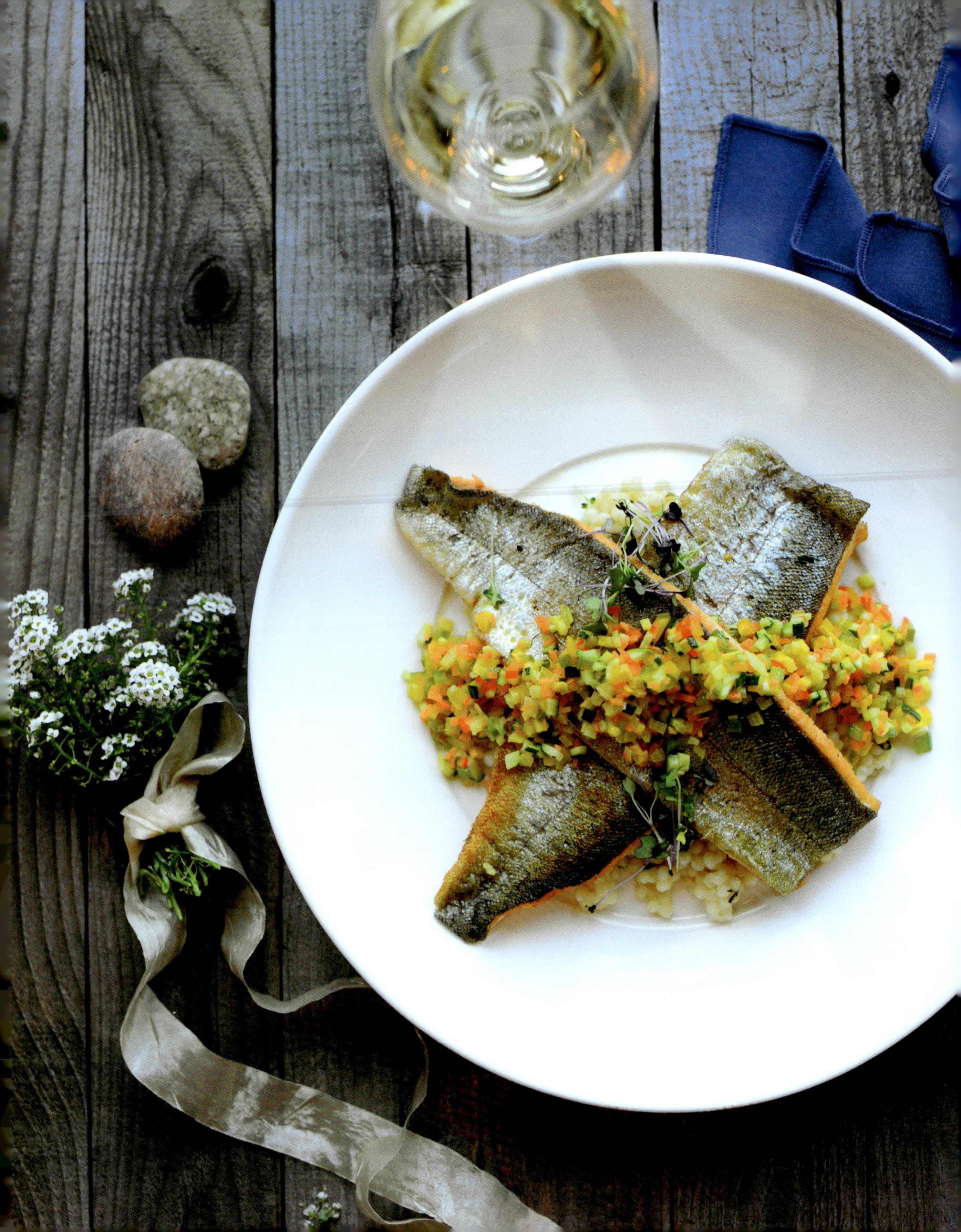

Pan-Seared Rainbow Trout with Minted Couscous and Brunoise Vegetables

Directions

Preheat oven to 350º F (175º C).

Couscous
In a medium pot over high heat, bring the stock to a boil. Add couscous and mint. Season well with salt and pepper.

Remove from heat, cover, and let stand for 15 minutes. Remove lid and fluff couscous with a fork.

Vegetables
In a medium skillet over medium heat, melt 1 tbsp butter. Sauté shallot until translucent. Add remaining vegetables, oil, wine, and lemon juice. Simmer until liquid is reduced by three-quarters.

Add lemons, herbs, and capers and simmer for 1 minute. Reduce heat to very low and add remaining butter, whisking until incorporated. Do not allow the butter to bubble, as this will prevent it from emulsifying. Season with salt and pepper.

Trout
If working with a whole trout, fillet and debone the two fillets of trout, then pat dry with paper towel. If you are using fillets, simply pat dry.

Make three small incisions in the skin of each fillet. This will prevent the fillet from curling when placed in the skillet.

Dredge fillets in flour and season well with salt and pepper.

Heat oil in a medium oven-proof skillet, over high heat. Add fillets and cook, skin side down, for 3 minutes, or until skin is crisp. Turn fillets over and place skillet in oven to finish for 8 minutes. Remove from oven and allow to rest.

Assembly
Spoon couscous into the middle of the plate. Place fillet on top, skin side up. Spoon vegetables and butter sauce over trout. Garnish with edible flowers or microgreens.

Makes 2 servings.

Ingredients

Minted Couscous
2 cups light fish stock or chicken stock
2 cups couscous
3 sprigs of mint, chopped
Salt and pepper, to taste

Brunoise Vegetables
3 tbsp butter, divided
1 tsp finely chopped shallot
½ yellow bell pepper, finely diced
½ red bell pepper, finely diced
2 oz carrot, finely diced
2 oz green zucchini, finely diced
2 oz yellow zucchini, finely diced
1 oz vegetable oil
2 oz white wine
Juice of 1 lemon
4 lemon segments
2 tbsp freshly chopped fine herbs
1 tbsp capers
Salt and pepper, to taste

Pan-Seared Rainbow Trout
1 whole rainbow trout, or two fillets of rainbow trout
3 oz all-purpose flour, for dredging
Salt and pepper, to taste
2 tbsp olive oil

Additional Ingredients
Edible flowers or microgreens, to garnish

The Naked Crêpe Bistro

Nicole Anderson and Chef Tom Stern

When Nicole Anderson and Tom Stern decided to open a restaurant in Wolfville they initially considered serving pizza. The popular food is simple, quick, inexpensive to make, and people love it.

But Wolfville is a university town, home to Acadia University, and it is already well served with pizza restaurants; so, instead, Anderson and Stern looked for something that would have the appeal of pizza, but with added flair. Crêpes fit the bill nicely.

"Crêpes are a versatile, easy-to-assemble, art form," says Nicole. "And you can make them as fancy or a simple as you want."

The Naked Crêpe serves both sweet and savoury versions of the thin French pastry. Three types of batter form the base — a standard flour-based batter, a buckwheat batter, and a batter made with chickpea flour. Both the buckwheat and chickpea versions are gluten-free, and the chickpea crêpes are also vegan.

Tom started cooking professionally at the age of 16, working in restaurants in Nova Scotia and other parts of the world. He and Nicole met when they were both employed at a Halifax restaurant. They decided to open their own establishment shortly after they married, five years ago.

Today, Tom makes his masterpieces in an open kitchen, for all to see. Every crêpe is made to order, and there is something to satisfy every craving. Breakfast crêpes, Thai, teriyaki, pesto chicken, salad crêpes, even "hangover" crêpes packed with ham, sausage, bacon, and poached egg — all are featured on the jam-packed menu.

Nicole calls it a healthy alternative to pub food. "We look at the things people love to eat, and we think 'How can we turn this into a crêpe?'" she says.

For the couple, The Naked Crêpe is a labour of love. "Tom loves to cook, and I love to eat," Nicole laughs. "We're a perfect match."

Lemon Curd Crêpes

Ingredients

Lemon Curd
Zest and juice of 2 lemons
4 eggs
½ cup butter or margarine
¾ cup white sugar
1 tbsp cornstarch
4 tbsp water

Whipped Cream
500 ml 35% cream

Crêpe Batter
1 ¼ cup flour, sifted
2 ¼ cups 1 % milk
9 large eggs
2 tbsp butter or margarine, softened
1 to 2 tbsp oil, for cooking

Garnish
Powdered sugar
1 lemon, cut into wedges
Zest of 1 lemon

Directions

Lemon Curd
In a medium pot over medium-low heat, combine lemon zest and juice, eggs, and margarine, whisking constantly, to prevent the egg from cooking. Add sugar and increase heat to high. Bring to a boil, whisking frequently.

Add cornstarch and water. Boil until thickened, whisking frequently, for approximately 2 to 3 minutes.

Remove from heat and allow the curd to cool, whisking occasionally.

Transfer curd to an airtight container and place in refrigerator. The curd will keep for up to 5 days.

Whipped Cream
Whip the cream in a stand mixer on high speed, until stiff peaks form.

Crêpes
In a medium mixing bowl, whisk flour, milk, eggs, and margarine, until smooth and frothy. Allow batter to rest for 30 minutes.

Heat a small amount of oil over medium heat in a large non-stick pan or well-seasoned crêpe pan. Add one-fifth of the crêpe batter and swirl to coat the bottom of the pan. Cook until lightly browned on the bottom, approximately 1 to 2 minutes. Carefully work a spatula around the edges and flip crêpe. Cook briefly on the other side, to set batter. Remove from pan and place on a piece of parchment paper, to avoid sweating.

Repeat with remaining batter.

Assembly
Scoop lemon curd into the centre of the crêpe. Fold crêpe into a pinwheel shape.

Garnish with whipped cream, powdered sugar, lemon wedges, and zest. Have fun with the presentation!

Makes 5 servings.

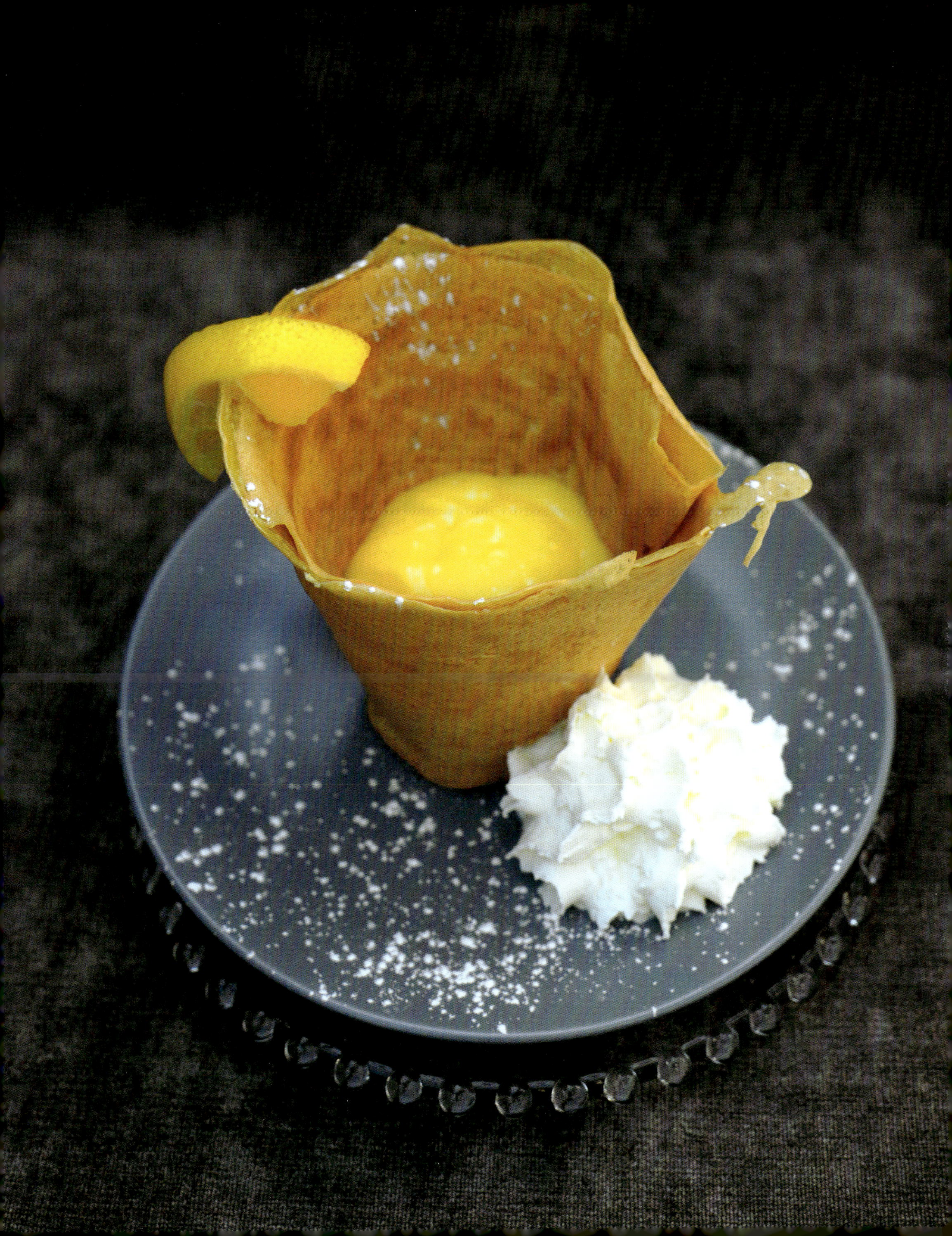

Divine Dishes Catering and Gourmet Take Away

Chef Nora Lindner

Chef Nora Lindner is on a mission to rid the world — or at least her neighbourhood — of bad food. The owner and chef at Divine Dishes Catering and Gourmet Take Away has spent her career creating foods that nourish body and soul.

"It's about more than just eating," she says. "Good, healthy food should be a top priority for everyone."

Divine Dishes is a catering company with a difference. In addition to preparing food for large corporate clients, gatherings, and events, the company also maintains a storefront that specializes in gourmet take away meals.

"Call it research and development," says Lindner. "In the catering business, we tend to make a lot of the same things over and over. With the storefront, we get to have fun. We can try new things."

Lindner and her husband, Peter Hiscott, opened the catering business in 2007, serving everything from simple corporate lunches for eight people, to plated meals for 300, and receptions for 500 to 600 guests. They added their Dartmouth storefront in 2015.

Today they serve a variety of take away meals: pizzas, pastas, salads, wraps, pastries, and baked goods, as well as complete dinner entrées. The menu changes regularly, with a heavy focus on local, in-season ingredients. Lindner calls it elevated comfort food, with a twist.

"I really do like the classics, but I also love the flavour bases of many different ethnic foods," she says. "My personal favourite is Thai because it has such a spectrum of flavours, but I love Indian food, Greek food; pretty much any type of ethnic food."

Lindner feels that no-one should take cooking too seriously.

"With a few very basic skills, everyone can cook. If there's something in a recipe that you want to change to customize it to your preference, give yourself the freedom to do that. Just trust your palate, and have fun with it!"

Left Nora Lindner, and Pastry Chef Angela.

Moroccan-Spiced Lamb Chops with Apricot Ginger Sauce

Ingredients

Moroccan-Spiced Lamb Chops
1 full rack of Nova Scotia lamb chops, separated into individual chops (7 to 8 pieces)
6 tbsp canola oil, divided (4 tbsp for the marinade, 2 for searing)
1 tbsp finely chopped fresh parsley
2 tbsp puréed fresh mango
1 clove garlic, minced
1 tsp finely grated fresh ginger
2 tsp ground cumin
1 ½ tsp ground coriander
1 tsp ground cinnamon
¼ tsp each of salt and finely ground black pepper

Apricot Ginger Sauce
1 cup apricot preserves (homemade or store-bought)
2 ½ tbsp white vinegar
1 tbsp finely chopped cilantro
1 tbsp grated fresh ginger
2 tbsp of water (adjust if needed)
Pinch of salt and pepper

Directions

Marinade
Combine 4 tbsp canola oil with parsley, mango, garlic, ginger, cumin, coriander, and cinnamon in a food processor. Season with salt and pepper.

Lamb Chops
Trim excess fat from lamb chops. Clean the bones with butcher twine. Rub chops with marinade. Marinate in the refrigerator for 2 to 24 hours.

Heat remaining 2 tbsp of canola oil in a medium skillet over medium-high heat. Add lamb chops and sear for approximately 3 minutes per side, or until 145º F (63º C) internal temperature, for a medium-rare cook.

Sauce
In a small saucepan over medium-low heat, combine all ingredients except water. Warm sauce through, then add a bit of water at a time, until desired consistency is reached. Use less water if you intend to use the sauce as a dip, or more if you plan to put the sauce directly on the plate.

Assembly
Plate chops and add sauce over chops (or serve sauce on the side, as a dipping sauce).

Makes 2 to 3 servings.

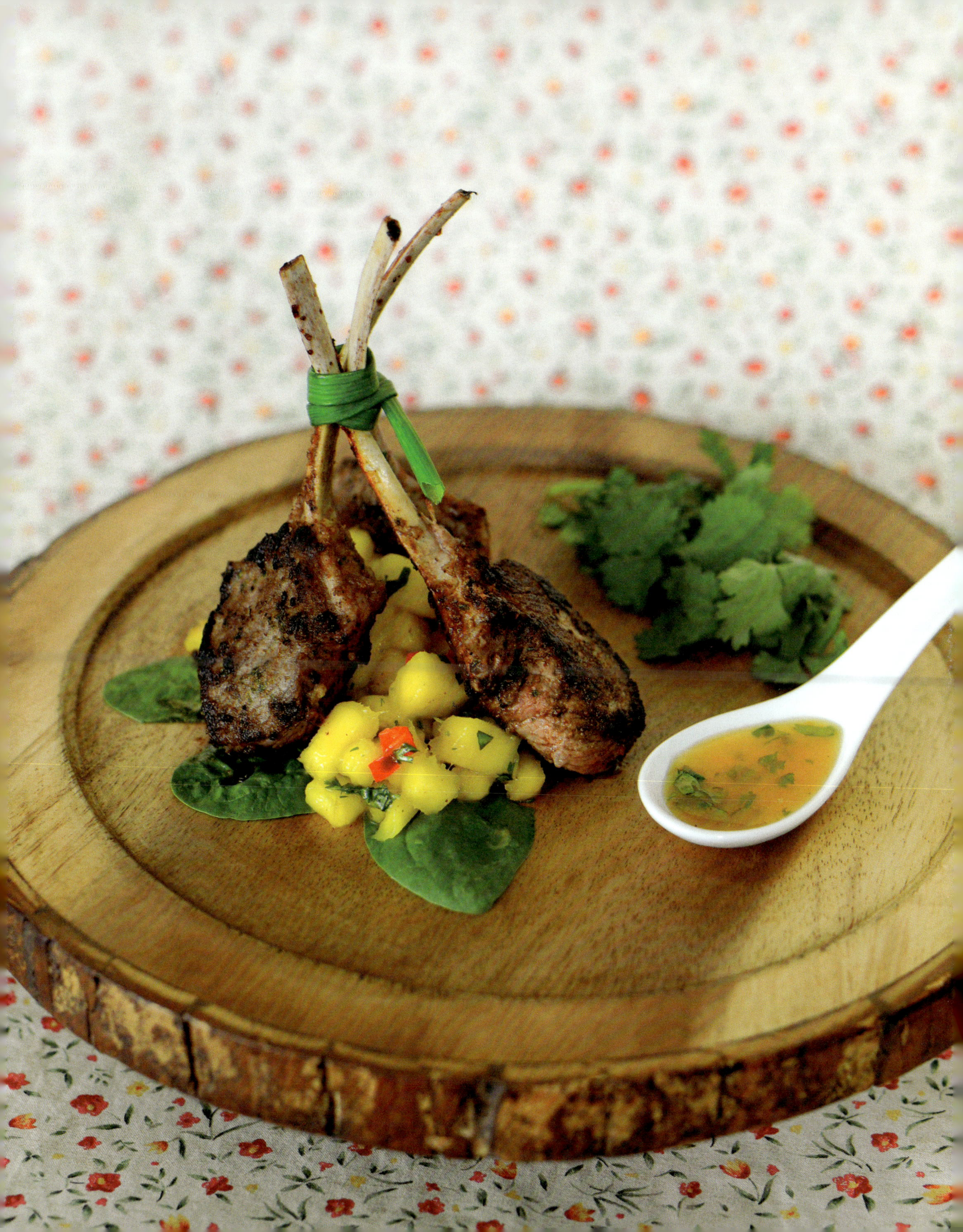

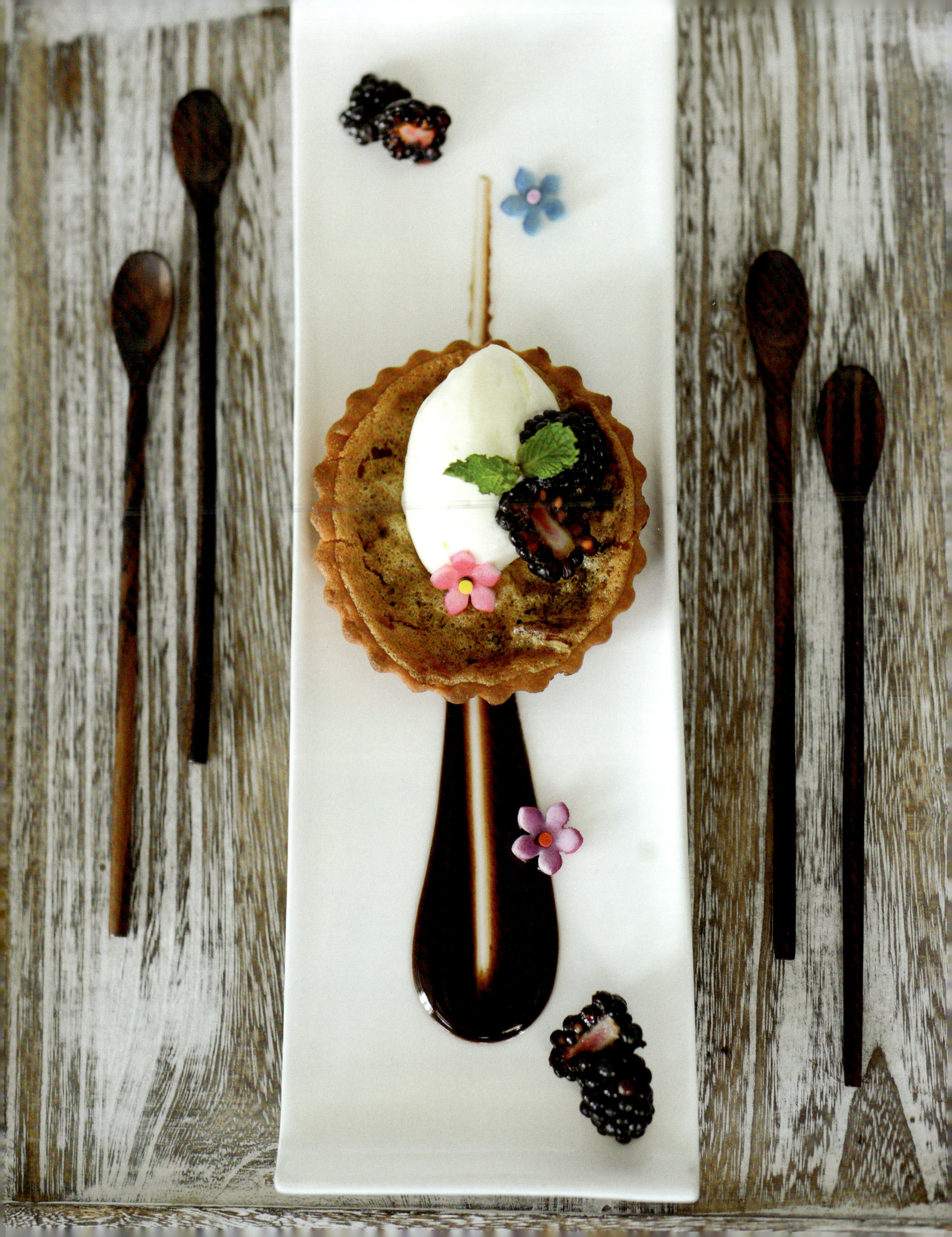

Chocolate Pecan Butter Tarts

Directions

Dough
Preheat convection oven to 350º F (175º C).

In a medium bowl, combine dry ingredients. Cut butter into dry ingredients until butter is pea-sized. Add wet ingredients and mix into a uniform dough. Wrap dough in plastic wrap and chill in refrigerator for 30 minutes.

Spray tart pans with cooking spray. Roll dough into tart pans. Place in oven and blind-bake shells for approximately 8 minutes.

Filling
Using a hand mixer, cream butter, sugar, salt, corn syrup, and vanilla. Add eggs and combine thoroughly.

Assembly
Preheat convection oven to 385º F (195º C).

Makes 12 servings.

Ingredients

Dough
4 cups (500 g) flour
2 cups (250 g) icing sugar
2 tsp (10 g) baking powder
1 cup (250 g) butter
1 egg
¼ cup (50 ml) milk
1 tsp (5 ml) vanilla

Filling
½ cup (120 g) soft butter
⅔ cup (140 g) brown sugar
½ tsp (3 g) salt
⅞ cup (265 g) corn syrup
1 tsp (5 ml) vanilla
2 eggs

Additional Ingredients
1 cup (175 g) chocolate chips
1 cup (105 g) pecan halves

Harbourstone Sea Grill and Pour House

Chef Trevor Simms

Chefs are storytellers as much as they are cooks, says Halifax Marriott Harbourfront executive chef Trevor Simms.

The stories that Simms likes to tell are about Phil, the Dartmouth farmer who grows the greens that he serves in his salads, and about the fisherman who pulled the restaurant's fresh scallops from Georges Bank at 4 a.m. that morning.

Simms' variegated purple, blue, and white carrots are featured on the plate to tell a tale that goes back to the days before carrots were selectively bred to be fat, orange, and somewhat diminished in flavour. He combines poached lobster with vanilla to illustrate how two flavours, harvested half a world away from each other, can come together in a delicious dish that makes perfect sense.

"I like to know where my stuff comes from," says Simms. "I try to make partnerships with great suppliers and tell their stories through the food I serve. Every restaurant has Digby scallops and local greens on their menu, but can they tell the story of the guy who grows those greens? I believe that's what people remember."

Simms loves experimenting with extremes in flavour and texture. His influences come from as far away as Asia, from his native Newfoundland and Labrador, and from the many restaurants he's worked in across Canada. Sharp, rich pomegranate molasses is one of his go-to ingredients, as is citrusy sumac from Israel. He even makes preserves in-house, to give his plates an extra zing.

Despite the unexpected flavours, Simms likes simple, descriptive menus that communicate the nuances — and the more exotic elements — of the dishes to his customers.

"I try not to use more than four or five ingredients, but the items that are in my recipes each have a place. I strive to tick all the boxes on flavour and texture. I want a crunch in everything, and I like to play the 'zone of your tongue' game: something sweet and something sour, balanced with salty."

A New Scotland Supper of Vanilla Butter Poached Lobster with Potato Chive Rösti and Roasted Variegated Carrots

Ingredients

Vanilla Butter Poached Lobster
1 ½ lb female Southwest Nova Scotia lobster
1 lb butter
1 vanilla pod
Nova Scotia sea salt and freshly cracked black pepper, to taste

Potato Chive Rösti
2 medium russet potatoes, grated
¼ cup caramelized onion
¼ cup chopped chives, separated
2 tbsp sunflower oil
Nova Scotia sea salt and freshly cracked black pepper, to taste

Roasted Variegated Carrots
2 lbs small variegated carrots, whole
1 oz pomegranate molasses
2 oz Cossman and Whidden honey
2 tbsp sunflower oil
Nova Scotia sea salt and freshly cracked black pepper, to taste

Directions

Lobster

In a medium pot, bring water to a boil. Season with sea salt. Add lobster and boil for 9 minutes. Remove lobster and allow to cool.

In a separate pot, gently melt butter over low heat. Split the vanilla bean in half and use a knife to scrape out the seeds, dropping them into the butter. Stir to incorporate seeds. Season butter mixture with salt and pepper.

Once the lobster has cooled, carefully extract the meat from the shell. Place in vanilla butter and continue to cook for 9 minutes, or until lobster is firm to the touch.

Rösti

Grate potatoes into a medium bowl and season with salt and pepper. Add caramelized onions and half of the chives, then mix with your hands. Hand mixing the ingredients will help to release the starch in the potatoes.

Heat sunflower oil in a cast iron pan or heavy skillet, over medium heat. Season the oil with salt. Drop in as many small piles of potato mixture as will fit in the pan. Press each down with a spatula. Cook until golden brown, then turn over. Continue to turn and cook until rosti are crisp. Remove from pan and drain on paper towel. Sprinkle with remaining chives. Season with salt and pepper.

Carrots

Wash carrots. In a medium bowl, toss carrots with pomegranate molasses, honey, and oil. Season heavily with salt and pepper.

Place on a baking sheet and roast for 20 minutes, or until brown and cooked through.

Assembly

Arrange lobster, rösti and carrots on a platter. Drizzle lobster with vanilla butter.

Serve family style.

Makes 2 servings.

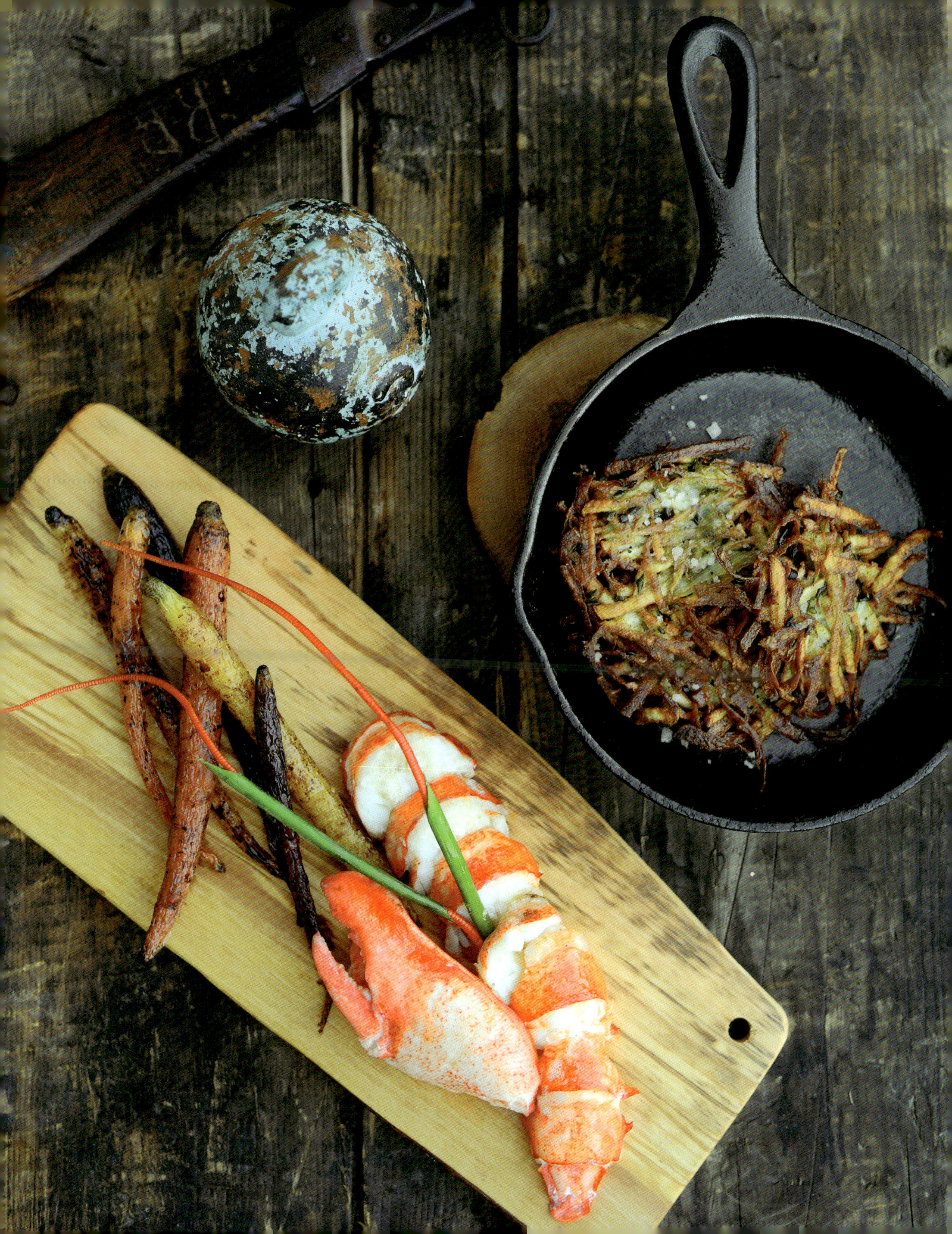

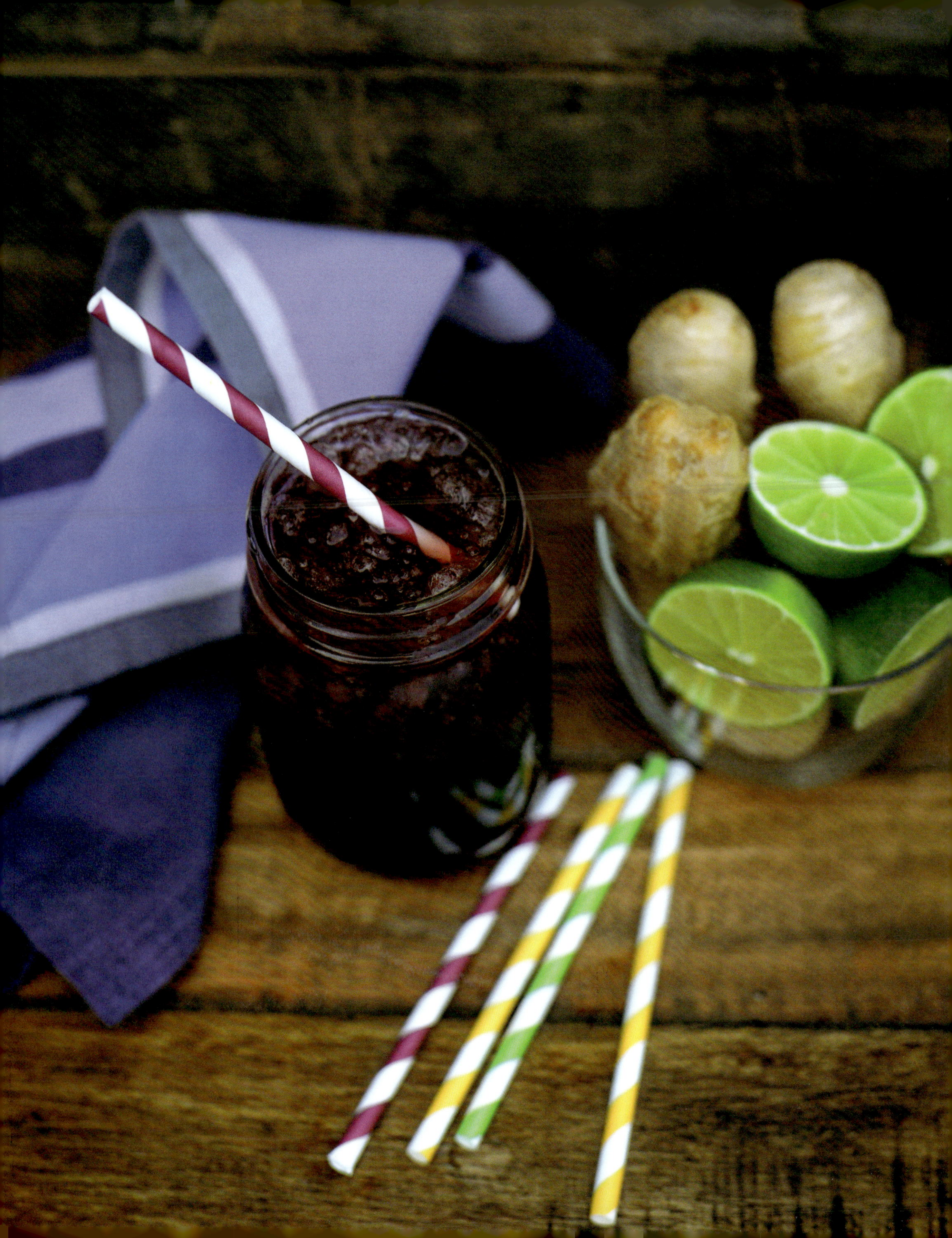

Spicy Ginger Summer Libation

Directions

Mix ginger beer, juice, and vodka in a shaker, over ice. Add a squeeze of lime, shake, and enjoy!

Makes 1 serving.

Ingredients

4 oz Propeller ginger beer
1 oz Haskap juice
1 oz Steinhart maple vodka
Ice
Lime

The Carleton

Chef Michael Dolente

The Carleton has long been a staple of the Halifax entertainment scene and became famous for introducing some of the region's best musical talent to the world. Many of the acts who cut their teeth on the Carleton stage have gone on to international success. The food, however, played a secondary role to the music.

Chef Michael Dolente has changed that. Since accepting the position of head chef in 2017, Dolente has rebuilt the Carleton's kitchen from the ground up, hiring all of the staff and completely redesigning the menu.

"It was a total overhaul," he says. "Today's menu is made totally from scratch. Everything is made in-house, with a focus on quality."

Dolente learned to cook as a child, at the side of his Italian grandmother. They made fresh pasta together, and she would send him home, proudly, with pasta and sauce for his family. He started his cooking career in high school, working part-time at The Cellar restaurant in Bedford — first as a dishwasher and then, after months of prodding the owners, with a position on the line as a salad cook.

He received his Red Seal chef certification in 2011 while working as an apprentice at a Halifax hotel. He later moved to Toronto and worked as a sous chef at several hotels, adding Asian cooking to his growing repertoire, along with French European style.

Dolente's recipes at the Carleton are globally inspired; an amalgam of everything he has learned. Today, prep work in the Carleton's kitchen has slowed down considerably. Stocks and sauces can take days to prepare, pasta is made painstakingly by hand, and ingredients are locally sourced and as fresh as possible.

"We don't take any shortcuts," he says. "Everything takes time, and everything we make is prepared with passion and care."

Fettuccine al Pomodoro

Ingredients

Fettuccine
1 ½ cups all-purpose flour
1 whole egg
7 egg yolks
2 tbsp olive oil
1 tsp kosher salt

Pomodoro Sauce
½ cup olive oil
5 large cloves garlic, peeled and smashed
½ small yellow onion, sliced thinly
2 (28 oz) cans San Marzano tomatoes
1 cinnamon stick
2 bay leaves
1 bunch basil (reserve a few leaves for garnish)
Salt and pepper, to taste
2 tbsp butter, at room temperature

Additional Ingredients
Salt, for pasta water
Parmigiano Reggiano, to garnish
Basil leaves, to garnish

Directions

Fettuccine
Place all ingredients in a food processor and pulse a few times, to make a crumbly dough.

If you do not have a food processor, the dough can be made in a large metal bowl. Place the flour in the bowl and make a well in the centre. Add the egg, egg yolks, oil, and salt, and whisk with a fork. Slowly start incorporating the flour into the centre. Continue until all the flour is combined with the egg mixture.

Turn dough out onto a lightly floured work surface and knead for 5 minutes, or until elastic and well combined in a ball. Cover the ball with plastic wrap and leave to rest at room temperature for 30 minutes.

Slice the pasta dough into 6 to 8 pieces. Run each piece through a pasta machine, starting at 0 and working up to 5 (or desired thickness). Fold the pasta over several times while running it through the machine, to help develop the gluten.

When the pasta has reached the desired thickness, run it through the fettuccine attachment. Dust the fettuccine with flour, and portion into nests on a floured baking sheet.

Pasta can be used immediately or frozen for later use. If you freeze the pasta, cook it from frozen - do not thaw.

Pomodoro Sauce
Heat olive oil in a wide saucepan, over medium-high heat. Add garlic and onion. Fry gently until golden brown.

Add tomatoes. Blend with a hand mixer or immersion blender, until smooth.

Add the cinnamon stick and bay leaves. Simmer on low heat for 2 to 3 hours, until tomatoes are fully cooked down, and the raw flavour is gone. Remove the cinnamon stick and bay leaves.

Add basil leaves. Blend with a hand mixer or immersion blender, until well combined. Season with salt and pepper.

If you are serving immediately, add the butter and stir until incorporated. If not, reheat sauce before adding butter. This recipe will yield approximately 6 cups of sauce, more than is required for this dish.

Assembly
Blanch the fresh pasta in simmering, salted water, until al dente, approximately 2 minutes.

Drain pasta and toss with a generous amount of pomodoro sauce. Plate into pasta bowls and garnish with freshly grated Parmigiano Reggiano and basil leaves.

Makes 4 servings.

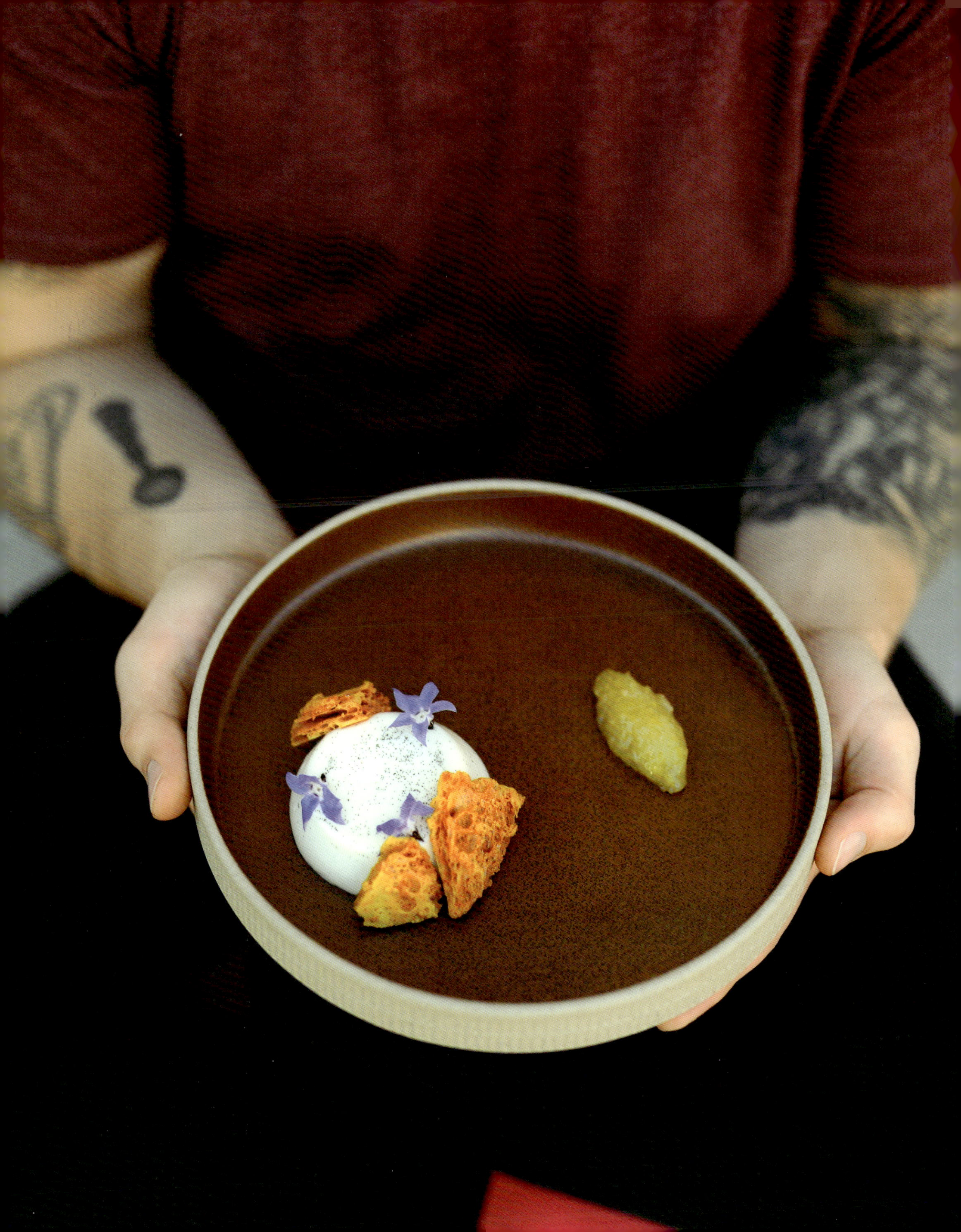

Vanilla Mascarpone Panna Cotta with Lemon Marmalade and Honey Sponge Toffee

Directions

Marmalade

Place lemon peels in a medium pot and cover with cold water. Bring water to a simmer, then strain the peels. Repeat this process 3 times, to remove the bitterness from the lemon peels. Cool peels and dice finely.

Combine the diced lemon peels, lemon juice, water, sugar, and pectin in a small pot over medium heat. Simmer for 20 minutes. Transfer mixture to a shallow container and refrigerate overnight.

Toffee

Combine the water, vanilla, sugar, and honey in a medium saucepan over medium heat. You will need a pan that is large enough to allow mixture to foam, at a later step. Simmer, without stirring, until lightly caramelized and temperature measures 300º F (150º C) on a candy thermometer. Whisk in baking soda. This will cause the mixture to foam.

Immediately remove the pan from heat. Pour toffee mixture onto a parchment-lined baking sheet. Do not spread or flatten. Allow the toffee to harden at room temperature, approximately 15 minutes. Break into bite-sized pieces.

Panna Cotta

In a medium pot over medium heat, combine milk, sugar, cream, and mascarpone. Whisk to combine. Cook for 5 minutes, to melt mascarpone and sugar.

Soak the gelatin sheets in cold water for 2 minutes, to soften. Add gelatin to the pot and whisk gently, until dissolved. Slice vanilla beans lengthwise and scrape out the seeds. Add seeds and pods to pot and stir. Turn off the heat and steep for 20 minutes to infuse the flavours.

Place a metal bowl over ice. Pour panna cotta mixture through a fine metal strainer into the bowl and stir gently for a few minutes. This will cool the mixture slightly and ensure that the vanilla beans do not settle to the bottom but stay suspended in the mixture. Pour mixture into 8 (3 ½ ounce) plastic cups and allow to cool for 4 hours in the refrigerator, or until set.

Assembly

To plate the panna cotta, invert the cup onto a plate, and carefully puncture a small hole in the bottom of the cup. Take care to avoid damaging the panna cotta. The hole will break the air seal. Press the cup into the plate and gently shake up and down until the panna cotta releases.

Garnish with lemon marmalade and honey sponge toffee.

Ingredients

Lemon Marmalade
Peels of 4 lemons
¾ cup (180 g) freshly squeezed lemon juice
¼ cup (60 g) water
½ cup (110 g) white sugar
1 (2 oz) (57 g) box pectin

Honey Sponge Toffee
⅓ cup (75 g) water
1 tsp (5 g) vanilla extract
¾ cup (260 g) white sugar
½ cup (200 g) honey
2 tsp (14 g) baking soda, sifted

Panna Cotta
1 cup (250 g) whole milk
½ cup (100 g) white sugar
1 cup (250 g) 35% cream
I cup (200 g) mascarpone cheese
2 vanilla beans
3 sheets of gold leaf gelatin

Makes 8 servings.

Horizons Catering and Spinnakers Restaurant

Chef Andy Thomson

Left Sous Chef, Raz and Head Chef Andy.

Don't tell Andy Thomson that cooking has limits. He hasn't found them yet.

"I've never believed in limiting my cooking to a particular style or cuisine," he says. "Great cooking is about making sure everyone at the table is happy, whether you're serving two people or 200."

Chef Thomson became interested in cooking as a young boy. The son of a single parent, he took on the responsibility of providing delicious, healthy meals for his sister and father.

Today, he runs Horizons Catering in Halifax and is the executive chef at Spinnakers restaurant at the Armdale Yacht Club, one of Halifax's oldest and most well-established yacht clubs. Horizons operates Spinnakers and provides catering for all functions at the yacht club.

Thomson works continually at improving his art; exploring new restaurants and sampling the work of other chefs, reading the latest cookbooks, and experimenting in the kitchen.

"I take a little from everywhere I can," he says. Indian cuisine is a particular favourite, and he loves working with fish, although he admits that it can be a complicated protein to get right. "I don't limit my cuisine to a few things. My recipes come from all over the place."

In a career spanning more than two decades, Thomson has worked across Canada in some of the country's best-known hotels and restaurants, under the tutelage of a number of top Canadian chefs, including Alex Clavel, Susur Lee, Mark McEwan, Mark Thuet, and Anthony Walsh.

Now, back in his home province, he loves to use the bounty of fresh ingredients Nova Scotia has to offer, including seafood from nearby Sambro, and meat and produce from the Annapolis Valley.

"I work as much as possible with local ingredients, but it has to be worth it," he says. "It has to be good."

Thomson focuses on technique and great ingredients to make his recipes stand out. He avoids using too many spices, preferring salt and pepper as his go-to staples.

"I like to keep things simple," he says. "That's the real secret to great cooking."

Seared Salmon with Acadian Maple Bacon Jam

Ingredients

4 (6 oz) salmon fillets, skin on
8 strips of bacon, finely diced
2 shallots, finely diced
2 oz Jack Daniels
¼ cup brown sugar
¼ cup Acadian maple syrup

Directions

Preheat oven to 350º F (175 º C).

Bacon Jam
In a medium skillet over medium heat, cook bacon until 90% rendered. Drain excess fat. Add shallots and simmer until translucent. Add Jack Daniels, brown sugar and maple syrup and simmer for 1 to 2 minutes. Remove from heat and allow to cool and set for approximately 30 minutes. Jam mixture may separate as it cools; mix well and reheat as required.

Salmon
Heat a well-oiled skillet over medium heat for 3 minutes. Sear salmon, skin side up, for 3 to 4 minutes. Turn salmon. Place skillet in oven for 7 to 8 minutes. Remove from oven and allow salmon to rest for 1 to 2 minutes.

Assembly
Plate salmon skin side down and top with bacon jam.

Serve with your favorite potato and vegetables.

Makes 4 servings.

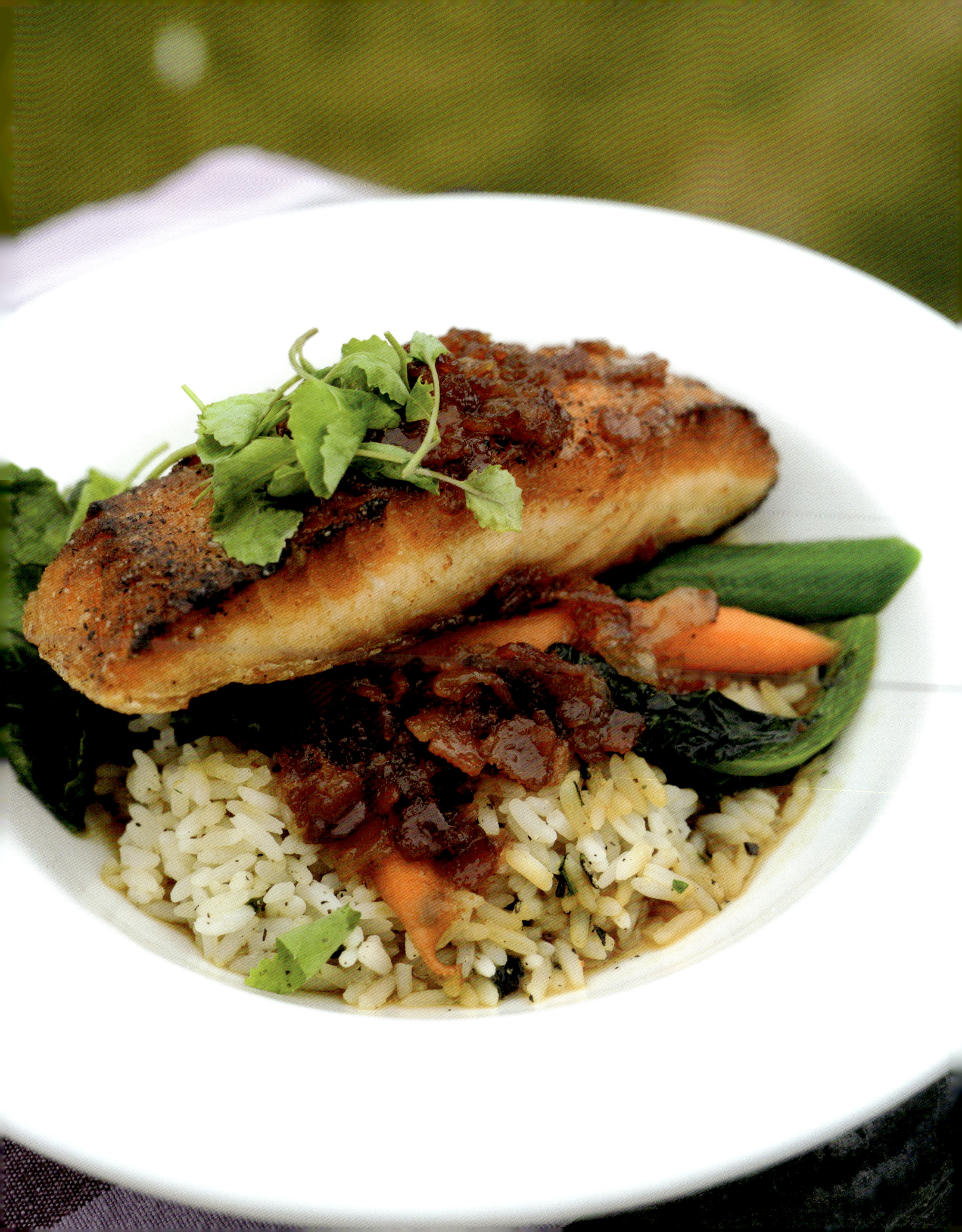

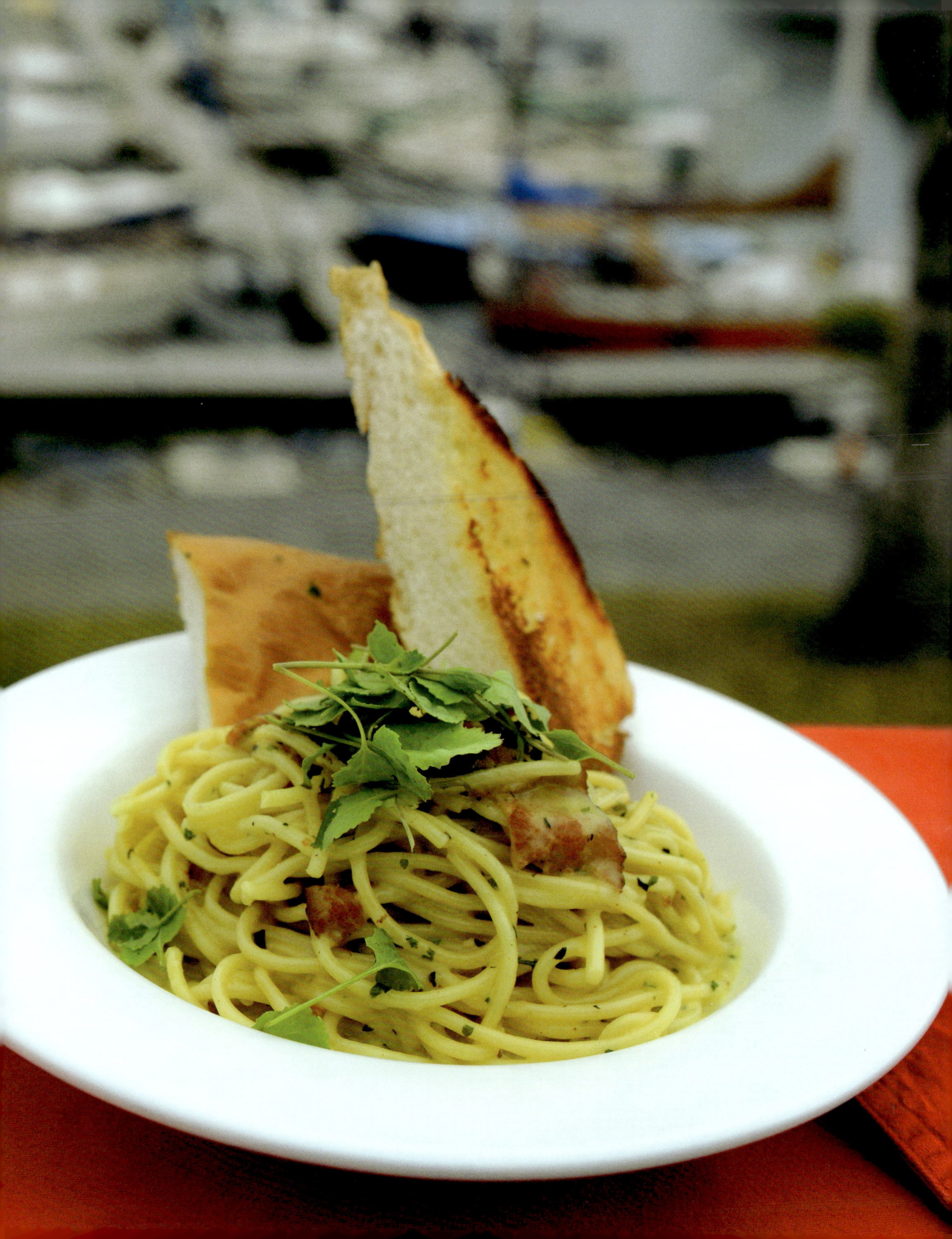

Spaghetti Carbonara

Directions

In a medium saucepan over low heat, cook the bacon and garlic until bacon is almost crisp. Add cream and simmer for 10 seconds, or until cream starts to bubble. Add pasta and heat through.

Combine remaining ingredients in a medium bowl. Add pasta and sauce and toss well.

Serve with garlic bread.

Makes 4 servings.

Ingredients

8 strips of bacon
2 tbsp minced garlic
¼ cup 35% cream
20 oz cooked pasta
4 egg yolks
¾ cup grated Grana Padano cheese
Pinch of fresh chopped herbs
2 tbsp coarsely ground black pepper
Salt, to taste

The Barrington Steakhouse and Oyster Bar

Chef Alex Jolin

Alex Jolin started learning to cook seriously at the tender age of 12. Soon afterward, the Quebec native set out to see the world. He travelled to places as far-flung as Corsica, Portugal, Hong Kong, Mexico, and Chile, funding his travels by working in restaurants along the way.

"I used cooking as a passport to see the world," he says. He ran an Italian restaurant group in Vancouver for six years, then a high-end fishing lodge in northern British Columbia, before eventually making his way to Halifax.

Today, Jolin is head chef at The Barrington Steakhouse and Oyster Bar in Halifax, where he has applied his global cuisine inspiration to create a unique flavour experience. Barrington Steakhouse goes beyond the expected, with locally sourced beef, fresh local oysters, a charcuterie board packed with items made in-house, and a hidden courtyard patio. On Thursday, Friday, and Saturday evenings the restaurant becomes a popular live performance venue for local musicians.

"Steak is our bread and butter here at Barrington Steakhouse," says Jolin, "but if I were to reflect on my preferred cuisine, it would be more Mediterranean in style. That is the type of cuisine I enjoy now. Very ingredient forward, a little less technique; just fresh ingredients, simply processed. You have to let your ingredients do the talking."

Jolin says that Barrington Steakhouse gives him a chance to explore his creativity in the kitchen, and his new Halifax home provides access to great local ingredients, including the fresh seafood that he enjoys working with.

"I love it all, from rolling out pasta by hand, to coming up with new ideas for the catch of the day," he says. "I take the best of whatever experience I can find, and I add it to my cooking repertoire."

Lemongrass Ginger Sea Bass with XO Sauce and Fennel Citrus Salad

Ingredients

Fennel Citrus Salad
1 bunch lovage, coarsely chopped
2 bulbs of fennel, shaved
1 lemon, juiced
1 lemon, segmented
1 orange, segmented
1 grapefruit, segmented
¼ cup olive oil
Salt and pepper, to taste

XO Sauce
8 oz dried scallops
8 oz dried shrimp
8 oz ginger, roughly chopped
8 oz garlic
1 lb ham, cubed
1 cup grapeseed oil
2 tbsp chilli flakes

Lemongrass Ginger Sea Bass
1 ½ lb whole sea bass
6 cloves garlic, finely grated
10 oz ginger, finely grated
½ cup grapeseed oil, plus additional oil to rub into fish
1 bay leaf
1 lemon wedge
1 sprig of thyme
1 stalk lemongrass
Salt and pepper, to taste

Directions

Salad
In a large bowl, combine lovage, fennel, and fruit. Season with olive oil, salt, and pepper and toss.

Sauce
Boil water in a medium pot. Add dried scallops and shrimp. Remove from heat and let sit for approximately 1 hour, to rehydrate.

Drain scallops and shrimp. Combine with remaining ingredients in a food processor. Pulse until smooth.

Put mixture in a medium saucepan and cook over low heat for 45 minutes, or until sauce is deep golden brown in colour and liquid is reduced.

Use sauce immediately or store in a sealed, refrigerated container for up to two months.

Fish
Combine garlic and ginger with grapeseed oil, to form a paste.

Stuff sea bass with garlic and ginger mixture, bay leaf, lemon wedge, and thyme. Skewer fish with lemongrass. Close with twine. Rub fish with grapeseed oil. Season generously with salt and pepper.

Grill over medium heat for 4 minutes on each side, or until skin is crispy and flesh is flaky and tender.

Assembly
Plate whole sea bass on a bed of shaved fennel and citrus salad. Garnish generously with XO sauce.

Serve family style.

Makes 2 servings.

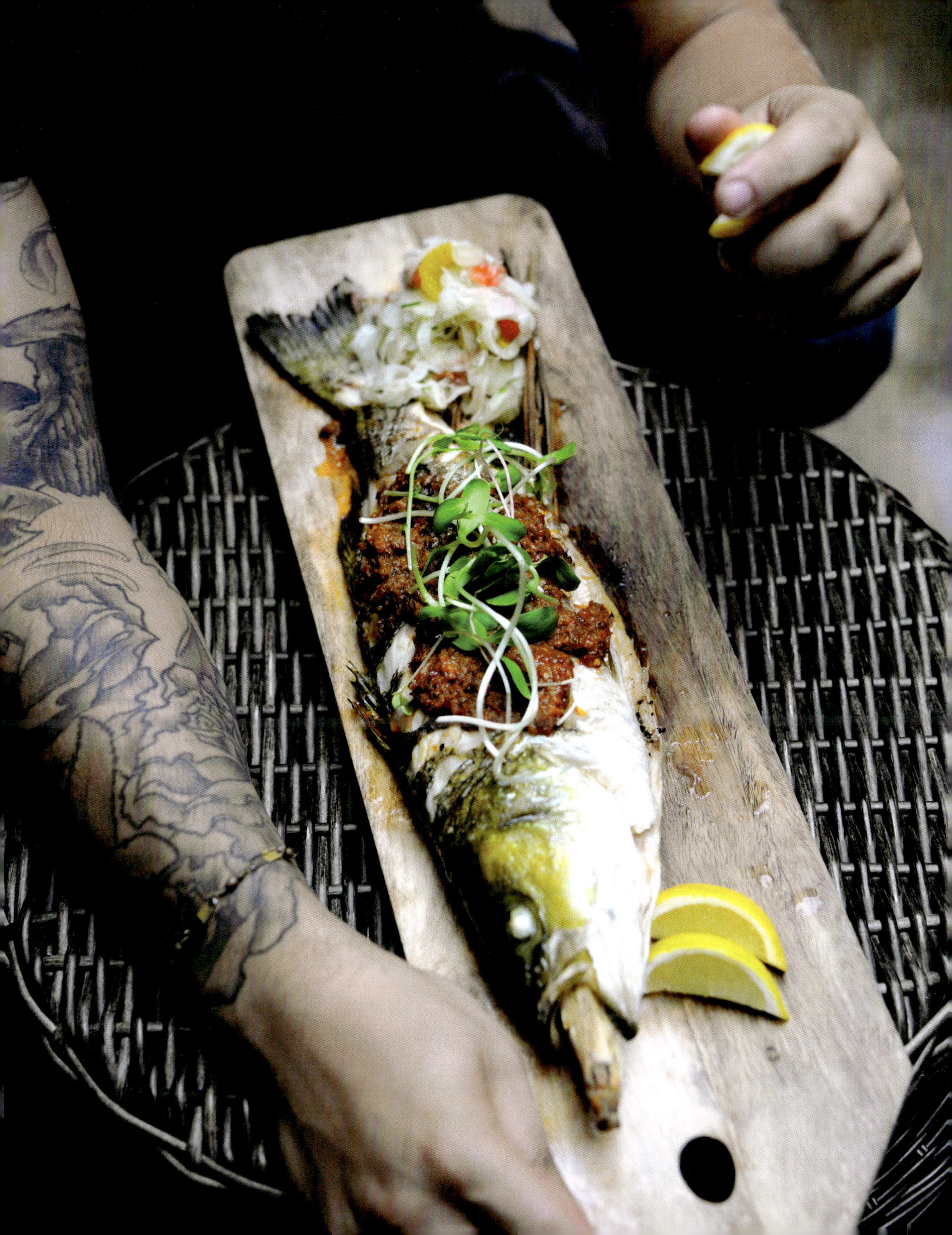

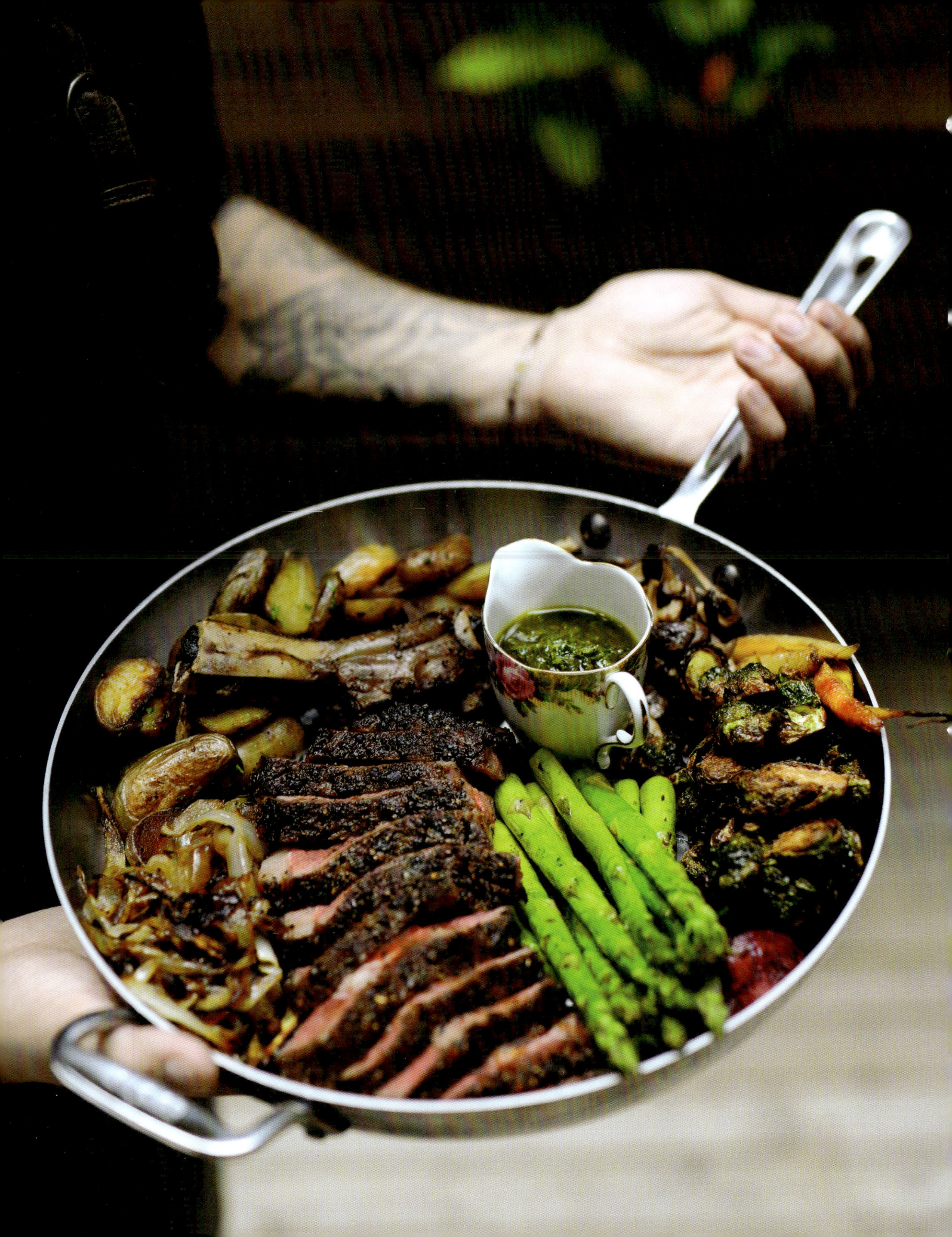

Côte de Boeuf

Directions

Preheat oven to 400° F (205° C).

Anchoïade
Combine all ingredients in a food processor. Pulse until chunky.

Beef
Preheat a cast-iron pan over high heat, then add canola oil. Season meat with salt and pepper. Sear on both sides until deep golden brown.

Remove from heat and place pan in oven. Turn meat every 5 minutes, until the centre temperature reaches 100° F (38° C).

Transfer pan from oven to stovetop. Add butter and rosemary and baste the meat, over medium heat, for 3 minutes.

Remove meat from pan and rest on a wire rack, tented in foil, until middle reaches 130° F (54° C), for a medium cook.

Assembly
Plate côte de boeuf on a large platter. Garnish generously with anchoïade.

Serve family style.

Chef's Note: At The Barrington, we enjoy serving our larger steaks family style, with roasted potatoes, grilled asparagus, mushrooms, and seasonal vegetables. The acidity and freshness of the anchoïade helps to cut into the richness of the steak.

Makes 4 servings.

Ingredients

Anchoïade
4 oz white anchovies
1 bunch basil
1 bunch flat leaf parsley
5 green onions
1 cup extra virgin olive oil
Zest and juice of 2 lemons
Salt and pepper, to taste

Chef's Note: White anchovies have a delicate lemony flavour. You can find them in most Italian grocery stores.

Côte de Boeuf
30 oz côte de boeuf (prime rib of beef)
½ cup canola oil
Salt and freshly cracked pepper, to taste
½ cup butter
1 sprig rosemary

Sushi Shige

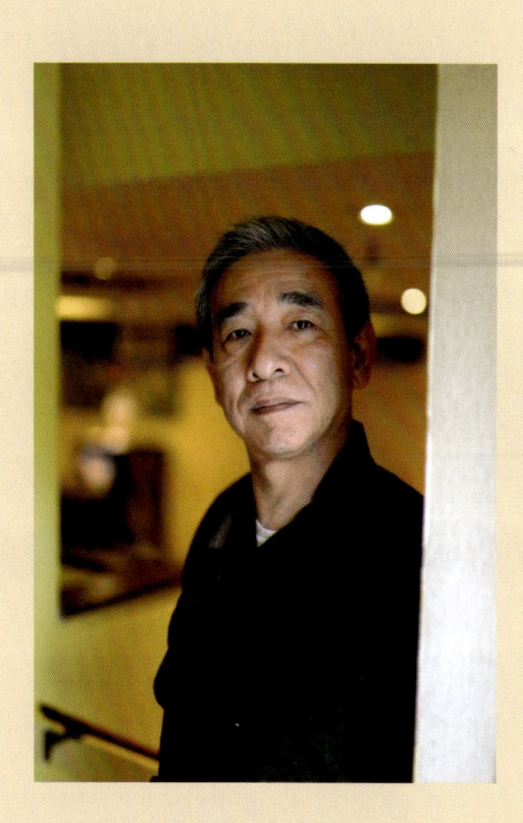

Chef Shigeru Fukuyama

For Shige Fukuyama, achieving the perfect flavour can be as simple or as complex as how tightly a handful of rice is pressed together.

It's the delicate balance of rice and air that influences the taste of each piece of sushi that the master meticulously creates at his restaurant in the heart of Halifax's Granville Street district.

"If you roll it tightly, when you put it in your mouth it tastes different," he says.

At his restaurant in downtown Halifax, Chef Fukuyama creates a palette of flavours that can't be duplicated by anything but his own practiced hand. His food is art that must be produced by a single artist.

"It's only my two hands," he says.

Fukuyama began crafting his masterpieces in his native Japan more than 40 years ago. "I loved to eat good food, so I decided to try to make it myself. That's how I got started," he says. He brought his craft to Canada in 1992, moving first to Toronto before discovering Halifax in 2000.

An evening at Sushi Shige is an experience that engages all five of the senses. In addition to sushi, the restaurant serves a broad selection of Japanese specialties, including tempura, teriyaki, and noodle dishes. All dishes are prepared in authentic, traditional ways, and each order is highly customized to individual taste.

Many of Shige's customers are regulars, and the chef works hard to learn the preferences of each one. He even customizes how the sushi are rolled - if a customer prefers to eat by hand, Fukuyama rolls the sushi more loosely; if they use chopsticks, he rolls it more tightly, as chopsticks work better with a tighter roll.

At the end of the day, Fukuyama's goal is simple. "There's only one thing we want everyone to do," he says. "Enjoy the food. That's it. If the customer is happy, I'm happy."

Temari Sushi

Ingredients

Sushi Vinegar
2 tbsp rice vinegar
2 tbsp sugar
1 tsp salt

Temari Sushi
2 cups cooked sushi rice
4 slices of smoked salmon
½ cup avocado, sliced thinly
½ cup cucumber, cut into thin strips
4 cooked shrimp, butterflied (sliced open to lie flat), with tails removed

Directions

Vinegar
Place ingredients in a small bowl. Whisk to combine.

Sushi
In a medium bowl, mix warm rice with vinegar.

Lay out a sheet of plastic wrap. Place 1 portion of salmon, avocado, cucumber, or shrimp on the sheet of wrap. Place a golf ball-sized portion of sushi rice on top. Twist the plastic wrap at both ends, to form a ball shape. Unwrap the plastic wrap. Repeat for each temari sushi ball.

Makes 16 pieces.

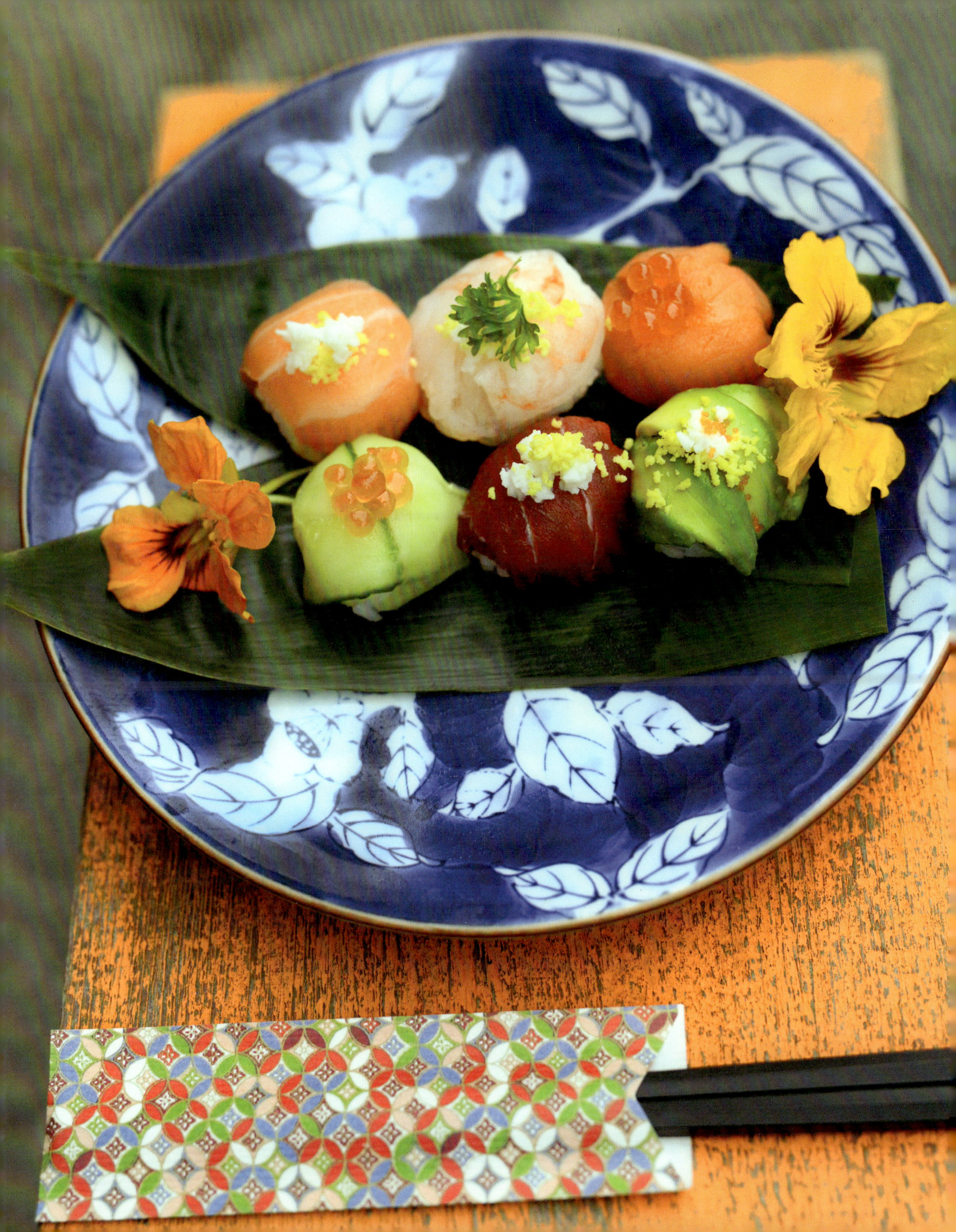

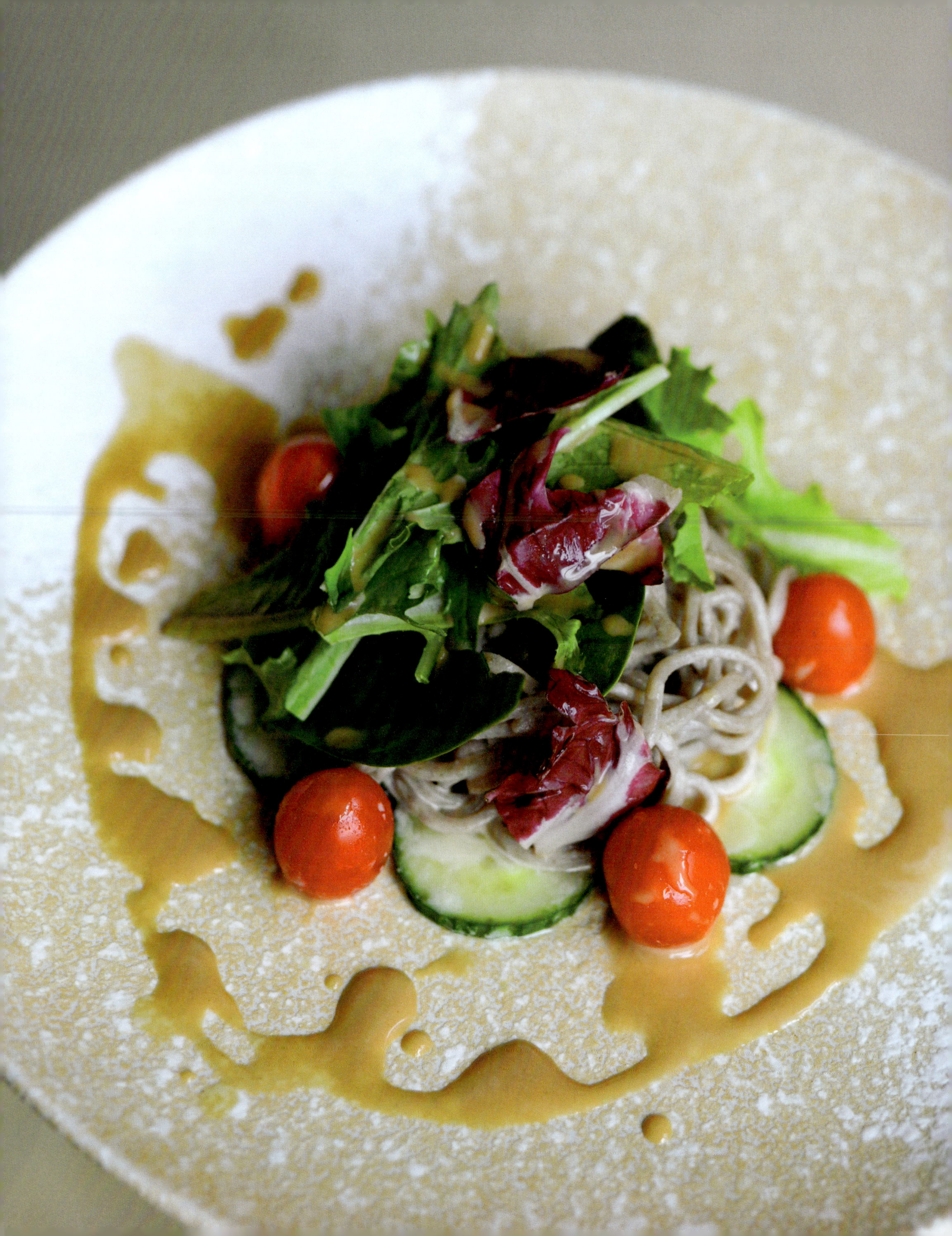

Soba Salad with Sesame Dressing

Directions

Salad and Dressing
In a medium pot over medium-high heat, boil soba noodles for 7 to 8 minutes. Rinse with cold water to cool. Drain well.

In a medium bowl, whisk dressing ingredients until well combined. Reserve ⅓ of the dressing for assembly.

Add soba noodles to dressing and toss to coat. Allow to marinate for 30 seconds.

Assembly
Place sliced cucumber on a plate. Top with marinated soba noodles. Add mixed greens. Garnish with cherry tomatoes. Pour reserved sesame dressing over salad.

Makes 4 servings.

Ingredients

Soba Salad
3 ½ oz soba noodles
1 ½ cups mixed greens
1 cup cucumber, sliced thinly
8 to 12 cherry tomatoes

Sesame Dressing
5 tsp sesame paste
5 tsp mirin (rice wine)
2 ½ tsp rice vinegar
2 ½ tsp soy sauce
½ tsp sesame oil

Le Bistro by Liz

Liz Ingram-Chambers

Liz Ingram-Chambers' approach to running a successful downtown bistro is a simple one.

"I love taking care of people," she says, "and having Le Bistro allows me to do that!"

This welcoming philosophy has helped make Ingram-Chambers' restaurant, Le Bistro by Liz, a staple of the Halifax dining scene; a popular establishment long known for French-inspired cuisine.

She started working at the original Le Bistro as a server in the 1990s, working her way up to the role of manager. After the restaurant closed in 2002, the space became home to several other ventures. With the dream of rebooting the bistro concept in her own style, Ingram-Chambers registered the name Le Bistro by Liz in 2007, then waited patiently. When the restaurant space became available in 2010, she quickly leased it.

Today, Le Bistro by Liz serves up casual fare with a French flair. Ingram-Chambers says she's elevated the menu to a healthier level by modifying some old favourites. However, in keeping with the French theme, she admits that they still use a lot of "wonderful cream and butter" in signature dishes, such as the restaurant's popular seafood crêpes and Coquilles Saint-Jacques.

Ingredients are sourced locally wherever possible and everything, down to the hollandaise and Bordeaux sauces, is prepared fresh, in-house.

"We're here to cater to the customers, not ourselves," she says. "If a diner has a specific dietary need and we have the means to make the necessary modifications to a dish, we will do it. I try to treat everyone who comes into my restaurant as if they are walking into my home."

It's a philosophy that she also imparts on her staff. "We're not just taking care of the client's hunger or thirst. It's more important than that. We're feeding their soul."

Coquilles Saint-Jacques

Ingredients

Potato
2 ½ cups russet potato, peeled and cubed
2 tbsp butter
2 tbsp 35% cream
Salt and pepper, to taste

Cream Sauce
2 shallots, minced
2 tbsp butter
2 tbsp flour
¼ cup white wine
½ cup 35% cream
½ cup milk
Salt and pepper, to taste

Mushrooms
3 oz fresh mushrooms
1 tbsp butter

Scallops
16 fresh scallops, 10/20 count (the large, juicy ones)
2 tbsp butter
2 tbsp oil
4 scallop shells

Additional Ingredients
1 oz green onion, chopped

Directions

Preheat oven to 350º F (175º C).

Potato
In a medium pot over medium-high heat, boil potatoes until tender. Drain and mash with butter and cream, until velvety. Season with salt and pepper.

Place potato mixture in piping bag with a large star tip. Allow mixture to cool.

Sauce
In a large skillet over low heat, sauté shallots in butter, until soft. Add flour and stir, to form a paste. Add wine, cream, and milk. Season with salt and pepper.

Increase heat to medium and bring sauce to a simmer. Whisk frequently, and simmer for 6 to 8 minutes, or until thickened. Set aside for assembly.

Mushrooms
In a separate pan, sauté mushrooms in butter over low heat, until soft. Set aside.

Scallops
When all other components have been prepared, sear scallops in butter and oil over high heat for approximately 2 to 3 minutes, until a light crust forms. Turn and cook briefly on the other side, again, until a light crust forms. Scallops should have a golden crust, but only be cooked halfway, as they will be finished in the oven.

Assembly
Place scallop shells on oven-safe plates. Pipe potato mixture into rosettes around each shell.

Place 4 scallops in each shell. Top with ¼ of the mushrooms and ¼ of the cream sauce, covering the mushrooms and scallops with sauce.

Place plates in the oven and cook for 20 minutes, until a golden crust forms on the potato rosettes.

Garnish with green onion and serve.

Makes 4 servings.

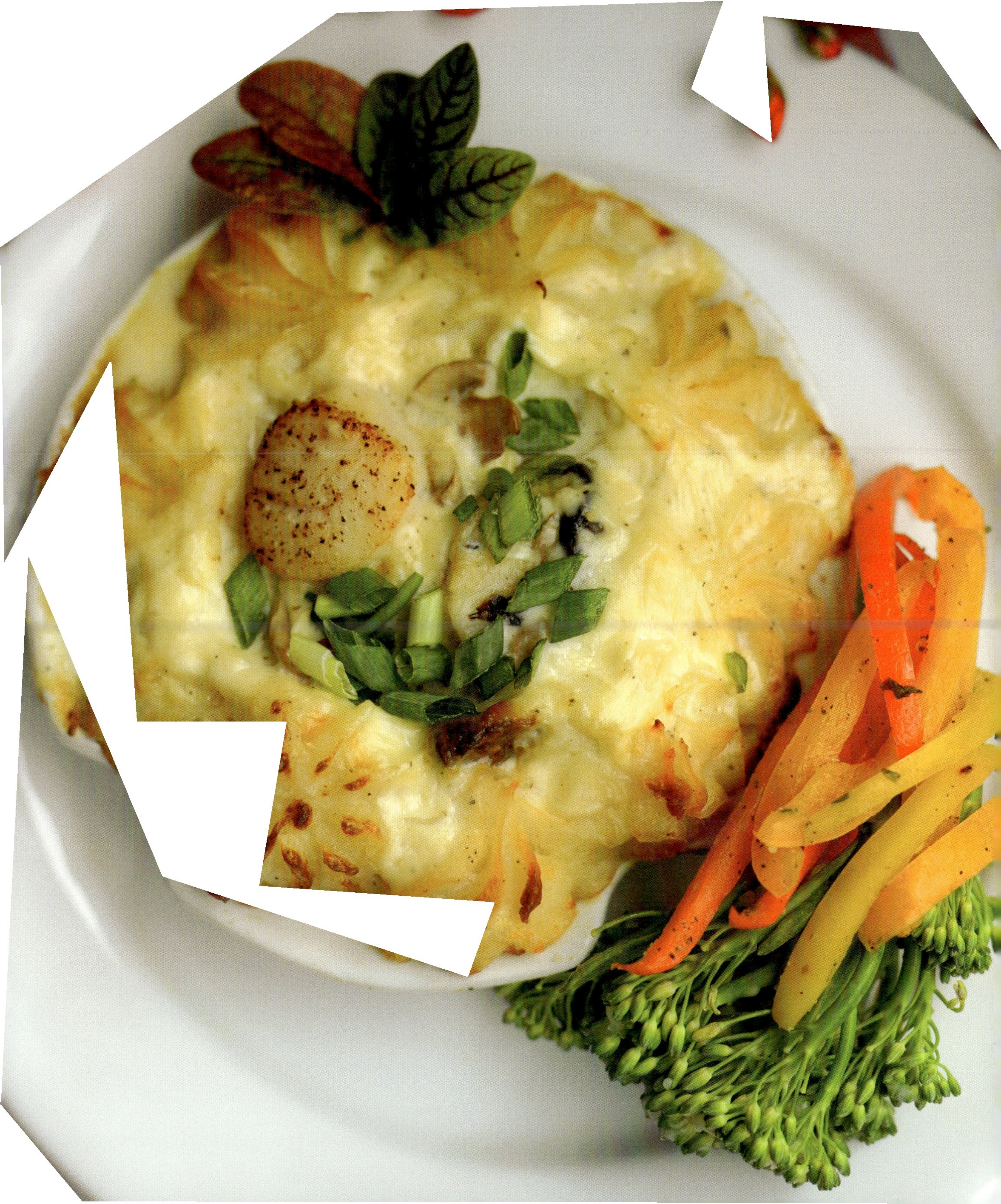

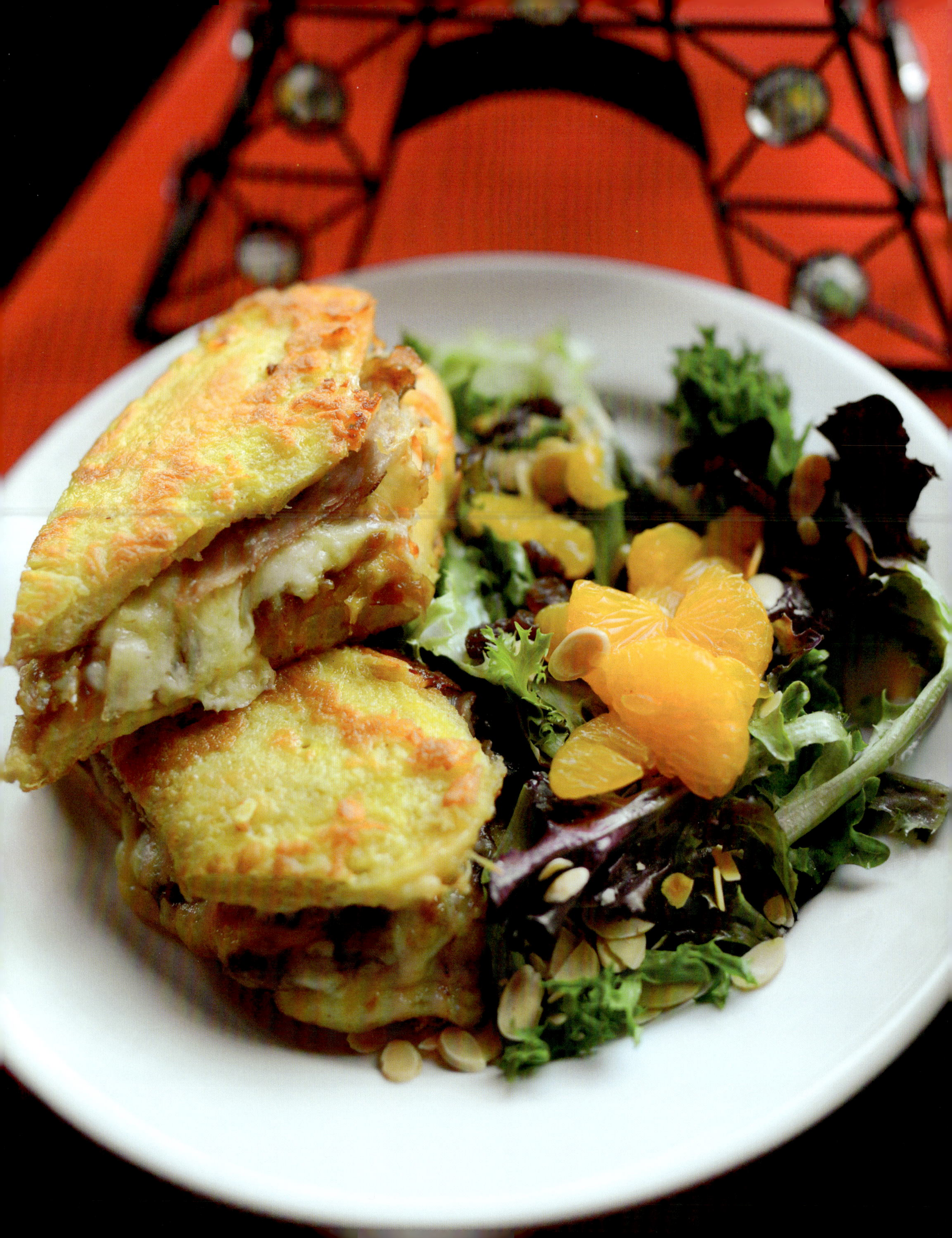

Croque Monsieur with Caramelized Onion

Directions

Preheat oven to 350º F (175º C).

Onion
Melt butter in a medium cast-iron skillet or heavy pot, over medium heat. Add onion and cook, stirring every 3 minutes, until golden brown and caramelized. Cooking time will be approximately one hour. Set aside for sandwich assembly.

For Each Sandwich
Slice off the top and bottom of the baguette, to create flat surfaces. Slice baguette in half, lengthwise.

In a large skillet, heat canola oil over high heat, to the smoking point. Remove skillet from heat.

Dip baguette pieces into whipped egg, then lay, flat side down, in the skillet. Put 2 slices of prosciutto on one piece, and 2 tbsp caramelized onion on the other. Top with ¾ cup grated provolone.

Place skillet in the oven for 3 to 5 minutes, until cheese is melted.

Fold baguette pieces together and cut sandwich in half, diagonally.

Makes 4 servings.

Ingredients

Caramelized Onion
6 tbsp butter
2 lbs onion, thinly sliced

Croque Monsieur
4 (6-inch) French baguettes
2 oz canola oil
12 eggs, whipped
8 slices prosciutto
3 cups grated provolone cheese

Ratinaud French Cuisine

Chef Frederic Tandy

Frederic Tandy likes taking his time and doing things right. That's a good thing.

Charcuterie isn't an art for someone in a hurry. In fact, the large cured hams that hang in the window of Ratinaud, Tandy's Gottingen Street shop, are the result of a painstaking process that takes more than two years — a month or more to cure, then two years drying in Ratinaud's 400 square foot drying room in the basement of the store.

The perfectly cured hams are a small part of a huge variety of charcuterie that Tandy creates in his shop. Sausages, pâté, rillettes, a variety of cured meats, foie gras, and his popular duck confit are featured in display cases or are hanging in the style of a traditional French delicatessen. The charcuterie products are complemented by fine cheeses that Tandy imports from Europe and Quebec.

Tandy grew up in France, a country with a long tradition of making charcuterie. He attended cooking school from the age of 15 to 19 and worked as a cook in his native country before applying for jobs in Spain, Bora Bora, and Canada in 2002. He received offers from all three places but chose Canada, and a cooking job located in a province he had never heard of before: Nova Scotia. "I fell in love with the place as soon as I arrived," he says.

Originally invented as a method of preserving meat in the days before refrigeration, charcuterie has become one of the signature culinary arts of France. The quickest product that Tandy makes takes about three weeks, with most charcuterie items taking a month and a half, or more, of curing, drying, and constant rotation.

Tandy's clientele ranges from well-informed foodies to curious newbies; he spends a lot of time educating them and introducing them to new charcuterie items.

"That's part of the fun," he says. "I love to share. Making charcuterie is my passion. It's a part of my life."

Cassoulet

Ingredients

3 cups Tarbais beans or navy beans
2 tbsp duck fat
2 Toulouse sausages
4 chunks of bacon or pancetta
½ medium onion, chopped
5 cloves garlic, minced
1 tsp tomato paste
½ cup white wine
6 cups duck or chicken stock
2 confit duck legs
2 sprigs of thyme
2 bay leaves

Directions

Soak beans in water for 24 hours.

Preheat oven to 300° F (150° C).

In a large, ovenproof pot over medium-high heat, melt the duck fat. Add sausages and bacon or pancetta and sear meat until browned. Add onion and garlic and cook until translucent. Add tomato paste. Cook for 2 minutes.

Deglaze pot with white wine. Simmer until wine reduces by half.

Drain beans. Add beans, stock, duck legs, thyme, and bay leaves to pot and stir.

Cover pot and place in the oven. Cook for 2 hours. When done, the stew will be creamy and the beans tender.

Makes 4 servings.

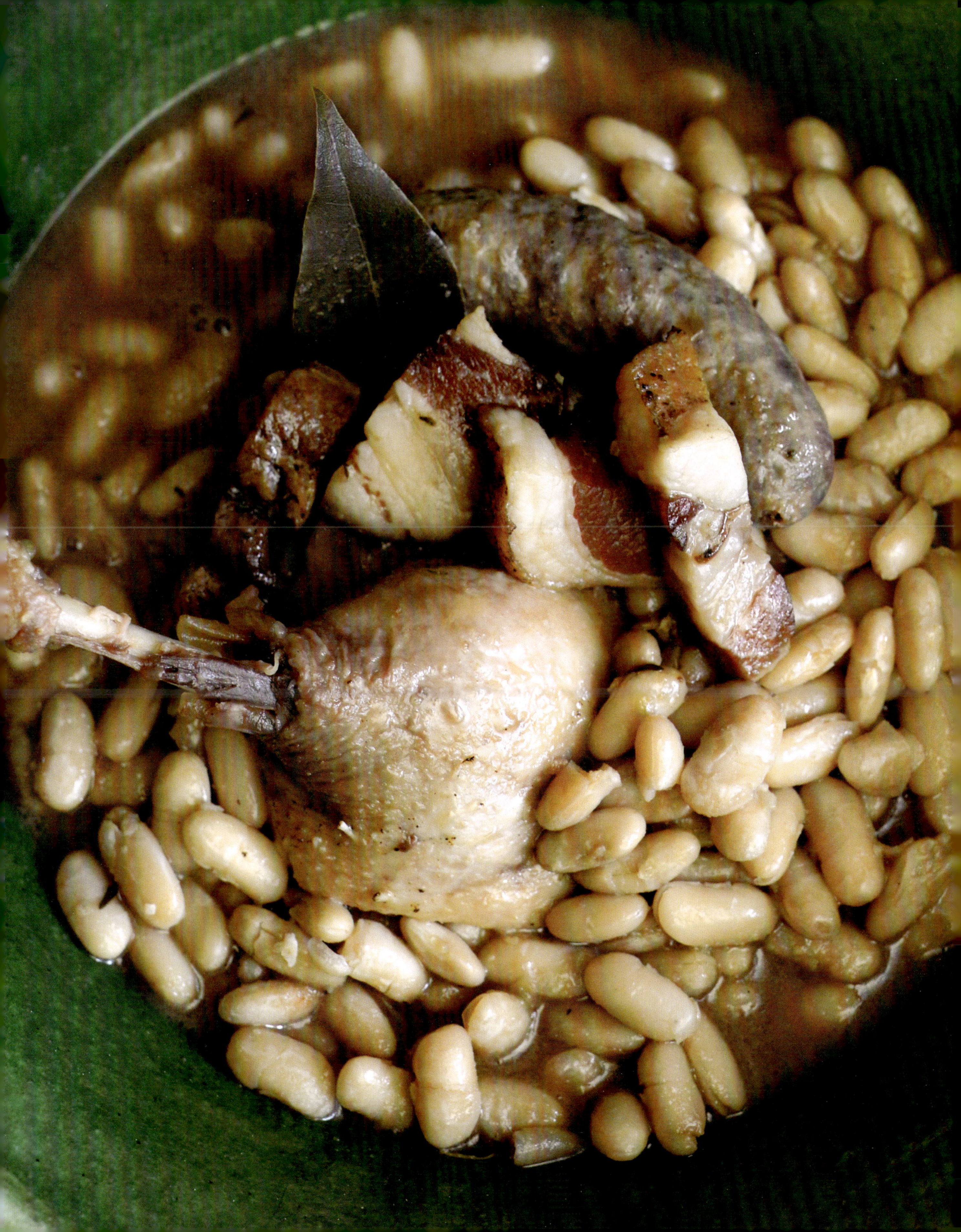

Pain de Campagne

Ingredients

Chef's Note: If you want bread for the evening meal, start the first dough by 3 p.m. the previous day.

Day One - Pâte Fermentée
1 lb (454 g) flour (Frederic uses half white bread flour and half wholewheat bread flour)
½ tbsp (9.3 g) salt
⅛ tsp (.35 g) yeast
1 ⅓ cups (298 g) water (should be a touch warmer than body temperature)

Day Two - Final Dough
1 lb (454 g) flour (same flour mix as day one)
½ tbsp (9.3 g) salt
½ tsp (1.4 g) yeast
1 ⅔ cups (380 g) water

Directions

Day One
Combine flour and salt in a bowl.

In a mixing bowl, gently sprinkle yeast into water. Allow to dissolve for 10 minutes. When the water is cloudy with yeast, add the flour mixture.

In a stand mixer on low speed, mix with the paddle attachment until ingredients are combined, then switch to the hook attachment. Mix for 8 to 10 minutes, or until dough pulls away from the bowl and forms a ball. The dough should smooth and elastic and somewhat sticky.

When you think the dough is ready, do a "window test." Pull and stretch a walnut-sized piece of dough, without tearing it, until dough is translucent. This translucency is called a gluten window. If you can stretch the dough without it tearing, this indicates that the gluten is well-developed, and the dough is ready to rise. The test will be different with every batch of dough, due to humidity. If the dough tears, add a touch more flour and mix again.

Place the dough in a large, oiled bowl. Cover bowl with plastic wrap and a towel. Allow dough to rise for a minimum of 16 hours.

Day Two
By 10 a.m. the next day, the pre-fermented dough should be "blown up," or risen, with large bubbles.

Make a dough from day two ingredients, using the same steps as day one, up until you are ready to switch to the hook attachment.

At that point, place pre-fermented dough on a floured counter. Using a knife, cut ping pong ball-sized chunks from the pre-fermented dough. Add these, a few at a time, to the dough in the stand mixer. Mix until all the pieces have been incorporated.

Continue mixing, stopping several times to check the "feel" of the dough. It should be somewhat sticky. You may have to add a small amount of flour at this stage, to make the dough pull away from the bowl and form a ball.

After about 10 minutes of mixing, the dough should pass the "window test."

Again, place the dough ball in a large, oiled bowl. Cover with plastic wrap and a towel and allow to rise for 2 ½ hours. Fold the dough over itself every 50 minutes. The dough should almost double in size.

When risen, place dough on a floured counter and cut into 2 or 3 equal pieces, depending on the desired size of loaves. Cover pieces with plastic wrap and a towel. Let sit for 15 to 20 minutes, to relax.

Uncover dough pieces. Shape loaves as desired. Cover again with plastic wrap and a towel and allow to rise for another 90 minutes.

When 20 minutes remain in the final rising time, heat your oven to 450° F (230° C).

Fill a spray bottle with water.

Line a baking sheet with parchment paper, and lightly sprinkle with cornmeal. When loaves have risen, place them on the baking sheet. Transfer sheet to oven, and immediately spray loaves well with water. Repeat 3 more times, at 30-second intervals. Spraying the loaves will help to form a good crust.

Bake for roughly 30 minutes, until the internal bread temperature measures 200° F (93° C).

Makes 2 or 3 loaves.

Lot Six Bar and Restaurant

Manager Sarah Amyotte

Terroir. The word describes the unique set of geographic conditions — climate, soil, the slope of the land — that give wines made in different regions their unique and distinctive flavours. It turns out terroir is also important for oysters, and Lot Six, a popular new restaurant and lounge in the heart of downtown Halifax, knows that better than most.

Lot Six features fresh oysters daily from around Maritime Canada — drawn from waters as diverse as Eel Lake, a tidal lake in southwestern Nova Scotia with 2.5 per cent salinity, to Malpeque Bay, Prince Edward Island (PEI), which has a full 3.5 per cent oceanic salinity.

"There is a massive difference between oysters from the north shore of Nova Scotia and the south shore of PEI," says Lot Six manager, Sarah Amyotte. "We serve three to four different varieties every day. They're typically fresh out of the water."

Andrew samples a specialty cocktail.

Cyle pours a warming beverage.

Teaching customers about different varieties of food and drink is something that Lot Six has become skilled at doing. Located in the oldest commercial building still standing in Halifax (the restaurant space was the sixth lot listed on the original blueprint), Lot Six attracts a lot of customers who are curious to know more about great cuisine. Amyotte and her staff are happy to educate them.

"We're constantly learning ourselves, and we love passing our knowledge on to our customers, whether it's information about oysters or charcuterie, or the latest wine or cocktail," she says. "We want our guests to have a great experience; we want them to be entertained, and we want them to leave feeling that they've learned something."

But don't think for a moment that an evening at Lot Six will be a pretentious or intimidating experience; quite the opposite, says Amyotte.

"Our food is approachable. There's not much on our menu that you wouldn't understand, and it's not the kind of menu where you would have to enquire about ingredients. We want everyone who comes in here to feel included, and to have fun."

Lot Six Mac and Cheese

Ingredients

Gratin Topping
½ cup panko breadcrumbs
½ cup grated Grana Padano cheese
1 bunch of chives, chopped

Mac and Cheese
1 tbsp butter
1 ½ tbsp minced shallots
1 ½ tbsp minced garlic
3 cups 35% cream
1 ½ cups grated Cows extra old cheddar
1 ½ cups grated Gruyère cheese
2 tbsp lemon juice
6 cups cooked macaroni noodles
Salt and pepper, to taste

Directions

Preheat oven to 400º F (205º C).

Topping
Mix ingredients thoroughly and set aside.

Mac and Cheese
In a large pot over medium heat, melt butter. Add shallots and garlic and cook until soft. Add cream, cheddar, Gruyère, and lemon juice. Cook over medium heat, stirring constantly, until cheese is melted. Add cooked macaroni noodles and combine thoroughly. Season with salt and pepper.

Assembly
Pour the macaroni and cheese mixture into a large ovenproof dish. Cover with the gratin topping. Bake, uncovered, for 5 to 10 minutes, or until topping is golden brown. Serve immediately.

Makes 4 to 5 servings.

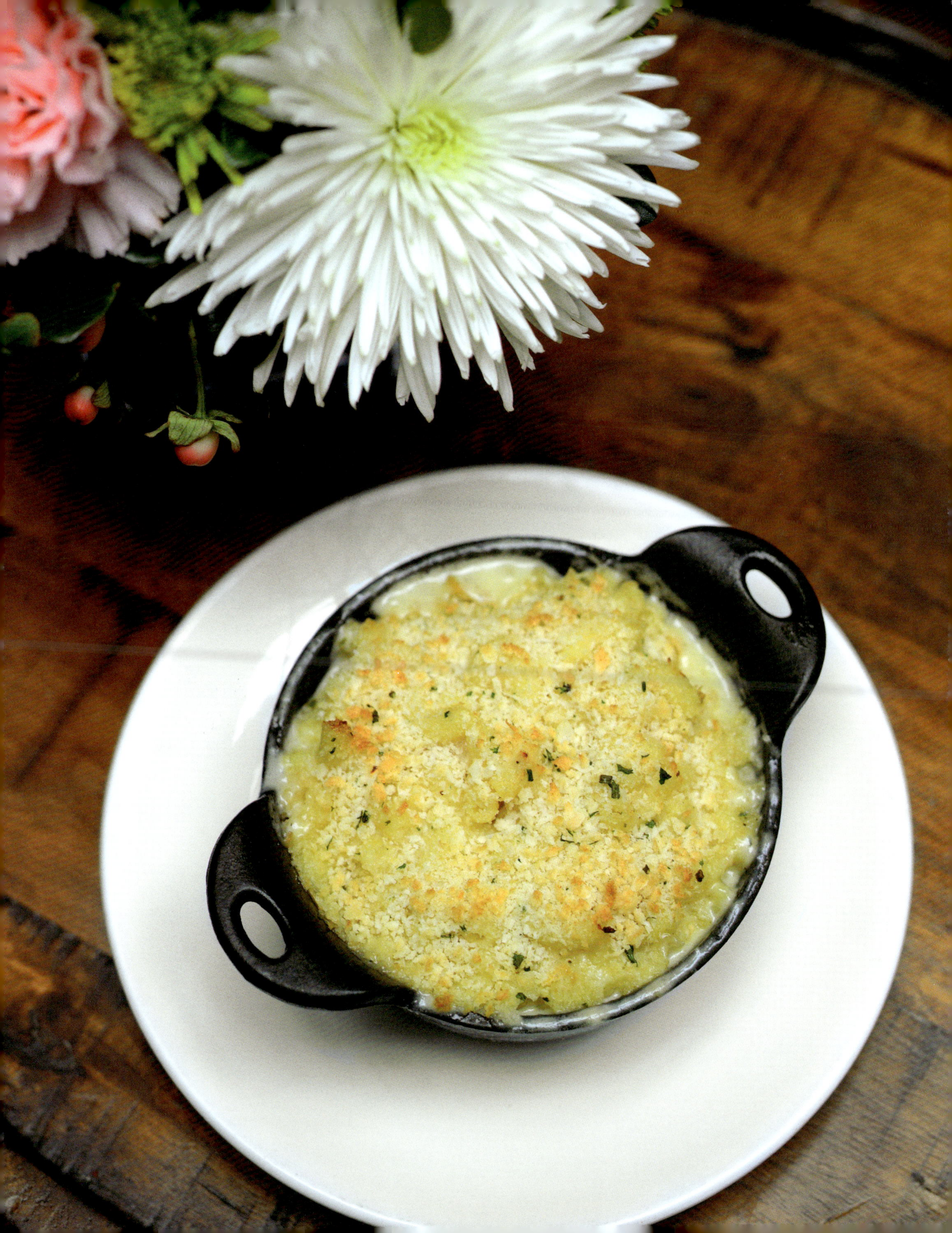

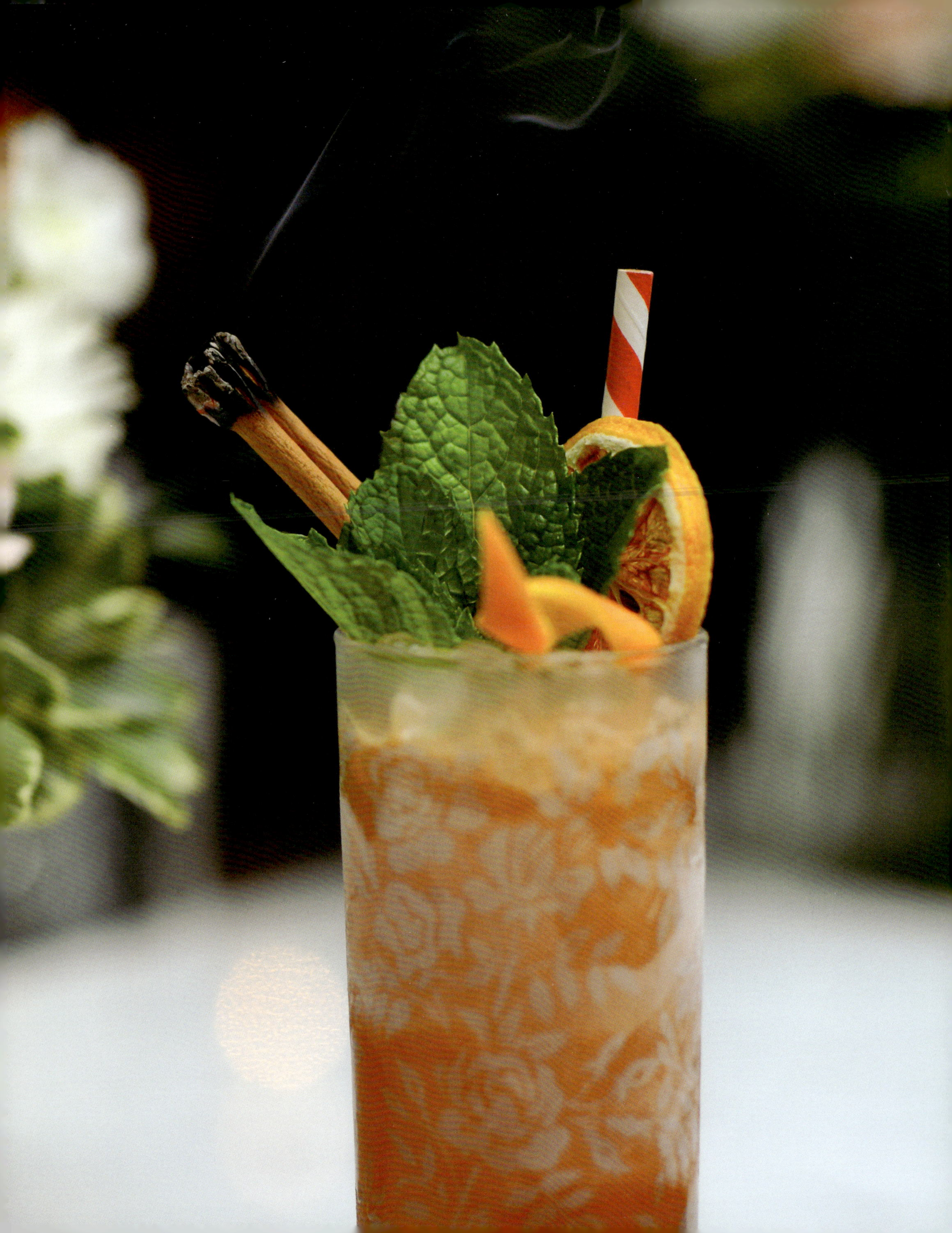

Magnum Moon Cocktail with Cinnamon Syrup

Directions

Syrup
In a small pot over high heat, bring the water to a boil. Add sugar and stir until dissolved. Reduce heat to medium-low. Add the cinnamon sticks and simmer for 10 to 15 minutes. Remove the pot from the heat. Remove the cinnamon sticks.

Pour syrup into a bowl and refrigerate until cold.

Cocktail
Add all ingredients, except soda water, to a cocktail shaker. Add ice and shake hard for 10 to 15 seconds. Open the shaker and add soda water. Strain the cocktail into a highball glass with ice.

Garnish with grapefruit and mint.

Makes 1 serving.

Ingredients

Cinnamon Syrup
1 cup water
1 cup sugar
2 cinnamon sticks

Magnum Moon
1 ½ oz bourbon
½ oz Cynar
½ oz fresh squeezed lemon juice
½ oz cinnamon syrup
2 dashes of Angostura bitters
Ice
2 oz soda water

Additional Ingredients
Grapefruit segments, to garnish
Mint sprigs, to garnish

Chef Abod Café and Catering

Chef Abod

Abdul Kader Sadieh doesn't want his customers to get too complacent about Middle Eastern cuisine.

Sadieh, who is also known by his nickname – and business name - "Chef Abod," says that the region where he hails from offers a far more complex selection than the kebabs and barbecue that most North Americans are familiar with.

At his restaurant in Halifax's north end, Chef Abod serves up dishes from across the Middle East, with spices and flavours as diverse as the mountains of Yemen are from the red deserts of Morocco or the ancient cities of Lebanon and Iraq. It's a skill he learned in his native Syria, working during the summer with his father — a professional chef — starting at the age of nine.

After graduating from cooking school, he honed his prowess in five-star restaurants in Bahrain, and later in Saudi Arabia as the personal chef of a Saudi prince.

Sadieh immigrated to Canada in 2011. He settled in Halifax and quickly realized that he needed to do something to stand out from the myriad of donair, shawarma and falafel restaurants that already populated the city.

"I decided to do traditional Middle Eastern food. I chose a well-known dish from each Middle Eastern country — from Lebanon, from Jordon, Syria, Iraq, Saudi Arabia, Yemen, Egypt, and Morocco. That made me unique."

To create his delicacies, Sadieh combines complex spices imported directly from the Middle East with fresh chicken, lamb, other meats, and produce, purchased nearby in Nova Scotia's Annapolis Valley. The result is a host of unique flavours and cooking styles.

At first, Haligonians familiar with standard Middle Eastern fast food didn't know what to make of the unusual offerings, but Sadieh has won over many converts to his cuisine. He estimates that more than 75 percent of his customers have no Middle Eastern background.

"When people try my food for the first time, they usually love it. Then the next week they come back with their friends."

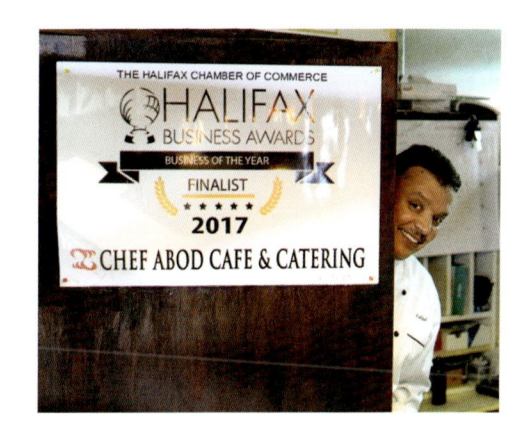

Fattoush Salad with Grilled Chicken Breast

Ingredients

Salad
1 ½ cucumbers, cubed
4 tomatoes, cubed
8 leaves lettuce, torn into small pieces
½ small onion, sliced
4 radishes, sliced
Mint leaves
Salt and pepper, to taste
Grilled chicken breast, sliced

Dressing
1 tbsp vinegar
3 tbsp olive oil
¼ tsp salt
1 clove garlic, minced
½ tsp dried mint
1 tbsp lemon juice

Topping
¼ cup pita bread, torn into small pieces
1 tbsp small black olives

Directions

In a medium bowl, toss salad ingredients.

In a small bowl, mix dressing ingredients thoroughly. Pour over salad. Toss again.

Plate salad. Sprinkle with olives and pita pieces. Top with chicken breast. Season with salt and pepper.

Serve family style.

Makes 2 servings.

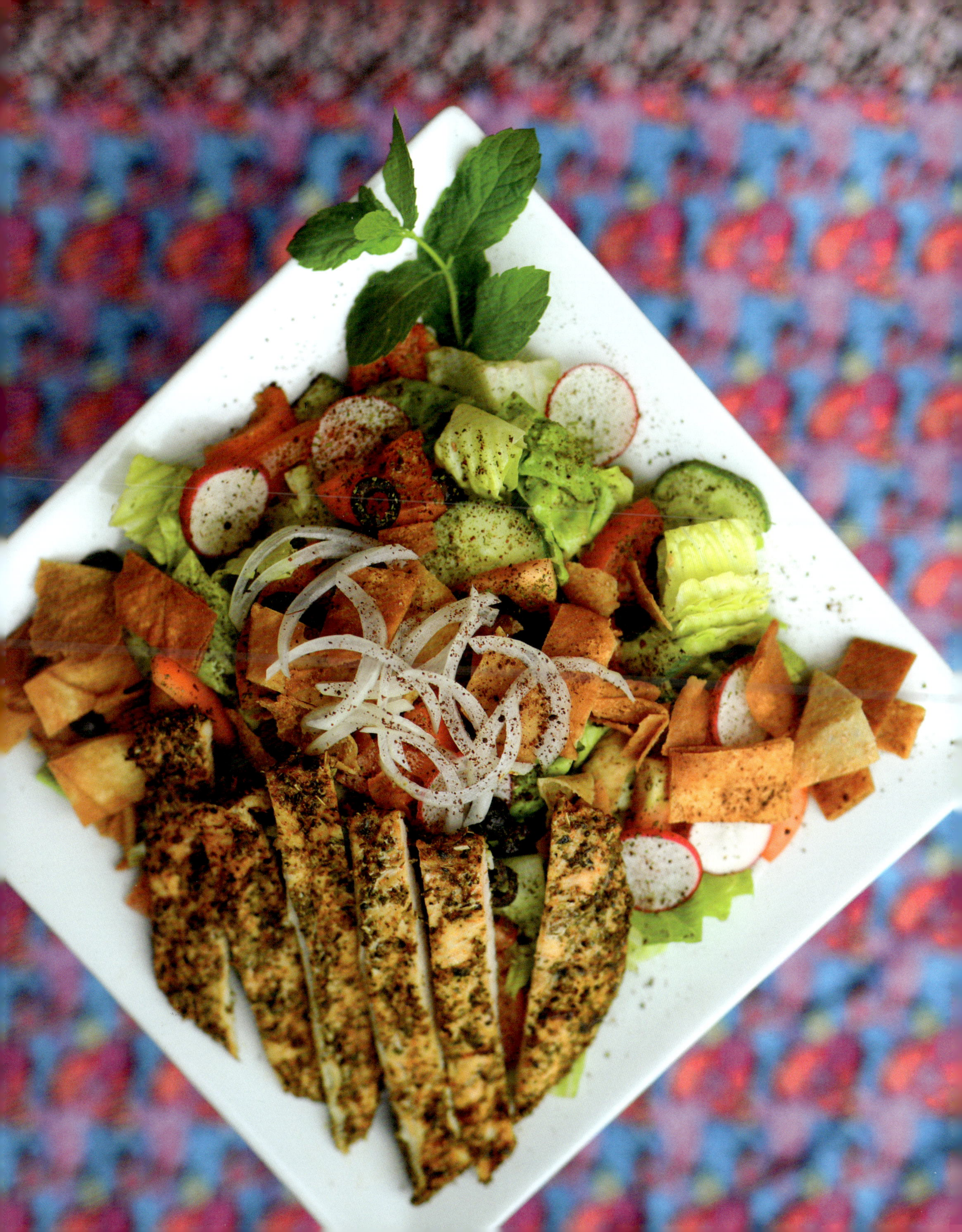

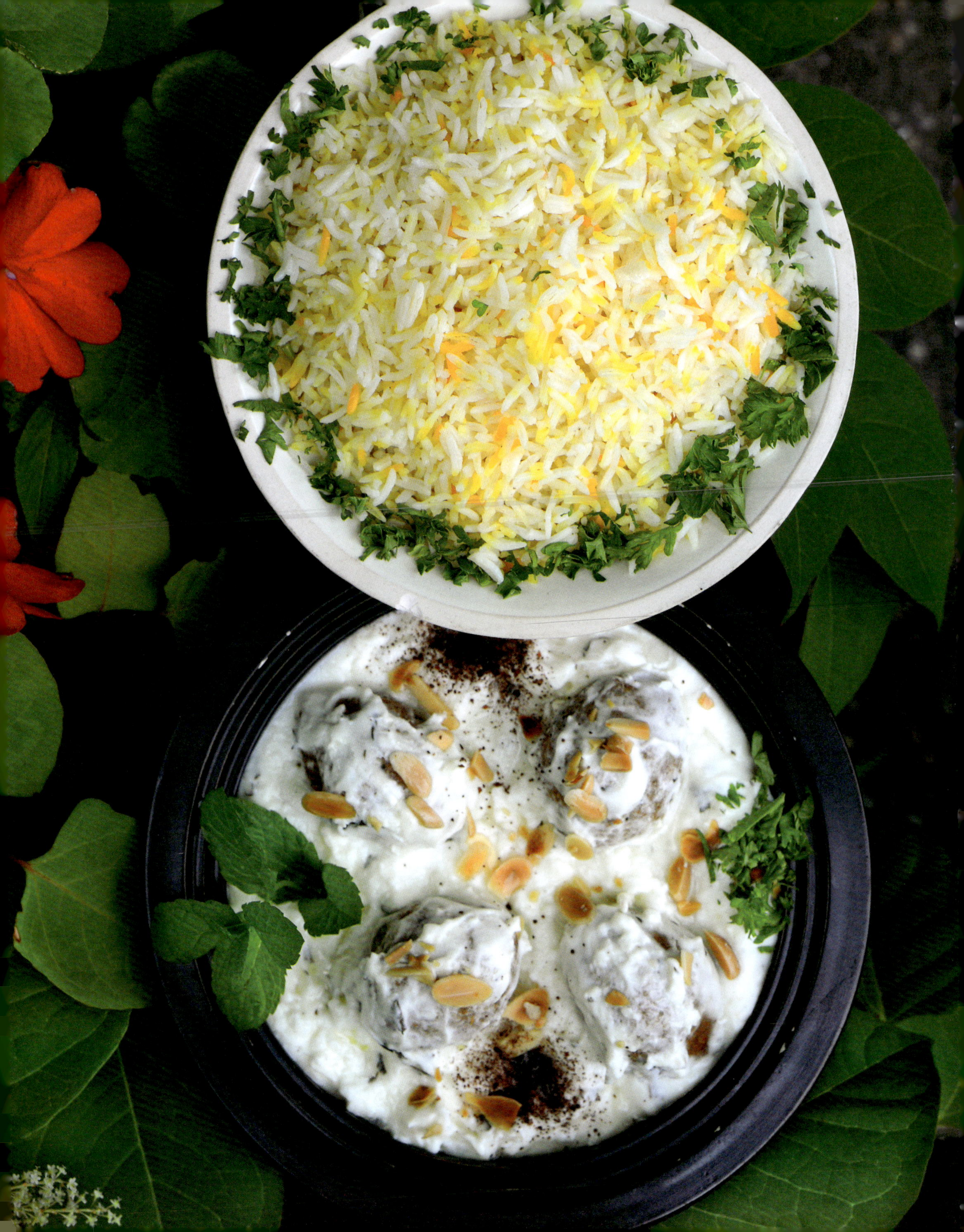

Kibbeh Lebaniah

Directions

Kibbeh and Filling
Rinse bulgur wheat several times with cold water, then soak for 10 minutes. Drain well and squeeze out extra moisture.

Using a food processor, mix bulgur with remaining kibbeh ingredients until well blended.

In a medium skillet over medium heat, combine filling ingredients and cook until well done.

In a large pot, heat water to boiling. Form a handful of kibbeh mixture into an egg-shaped portion. Make a hole at one end. Stuff with filling, then close the hole. Repeat for each kibbeh ball. Place kibbeh in the pot and boil for 5 minutes.

Yogurt Sauce
In a large saucepan over medium heat, combine yogurt sauce ingredients. Bring to a simmer and cook, stirring continuously to prevent sticking, for approximately 5 minutes.

Assembly
Drain kibbeh and carefully place in yogurt sauce. Simmer for an additional 5 minutes.

Plate sauce and kibbeh in a large, shallow bowl. Garnish with almonds and mint leaves. Sprinkle with sumac.

Serve family style.

Makes 3 servings.

Ingredients

Kibbeh
14 oz extra lean ground beef
3 cups fine bulgur wheat
1 medium onion, quartered
¼ tsp ground black pepper
½ tsp salt

Filling
18 oz lean ground beef
4 tbsp vegetable oil
1 tsp salt
½ tsp black pepper
¼ cup slivered almonds

Yogurt Sauce
3 cups plain yogurt
1 cup water
2 eggs
2 tbsp cornstarch
1 tsp salt

Garnish
Slivered almonds
Mint leaves
Pinch of ground sumac

Lamb Mandi

Ingredients

Lamb
4 lamb shanks
2 onions, chopped
6 cardamom pods
4 cinnamon sticks
4 whole cloves
5 bay leaves
Salt and pepper, to taste
1 carrot, coarsely chopped
4 oz ginger
4 tomatoes, sliced
4 cups water
1 piece of natural charcoal (available at natural food stores)
1 tbsp oil

Rice
3 tbsp oil
1 onion, chopped
2 cups rice
Salt, to taste
3 cardamom pods
1 cinnamon stick
4 cups water
Pinch of saffron
1 piece of natural charcoal

Caramelized Onion
2 tbsp oil
1 onion, finely chopped

Garnish
¼ cup raisins
¼ cup slivered almonds

Directions

Heat oven to 350°F (175°C).

Lamb
Place lamb shanks in a large roasting pan with all other ingredients, except charcoal and oil. Cover pan with foil and cook for 2 to 3 hours.

When the lamb is done, carefully fire one piece of charcoal directly on the element or stovetop, over high heat.

Make a foil cup, add 1 tbsp oil and the charcoal to the cup, and place it in the middle of the lamb shanks. Cover pan and cook for an additional 20 minutes. The charcoal will add a beautiful smoky flavour to the lamb.

Rice
In a large pot over medium heat, heat 2 tbsp oil. Add onion. Cook until tender.

Add rice, salt, cardamom, cinnamon, and water. Bring to boil, then reduce to low heat. Add a sprinkle of saffron, for colour and flavour. Cook, covered, for 15 to 20 minutes.

Fire the second piece of charcoal over high heat. Make a foil cup, add 1 tbsp oil and the charcoal to the cup, and place it in the middle of the rice. Remove pot from heat, cover, and let sit for 10 minutes.

Onion
In a small skillet over medium-low heat, fry onion in 2 tbsp oil, until caramelized.

Assembly
To serve, scoop rice onto a large platter. Top with lamb shanks. Sprinkle caramelized onion, raisins, and almonds around the edge.

Serve family style.

Makes 4 servings.